MathFlare

Name: ______________________

Class: ___________

Teacher: ______________________

Introduction

As parents and educators, we recognize the pivotal role mathematics plays in shaping a child's academic journey and future success. Yet, the path to mathematical proficiency can often seem daunting, fraught with challenges and complexities. That's where the transformative power of MathFlare Workbooks shine through, illuminating the way forward with clarity, precision, and purpose.

Introducing MathFlare Workbooks – a beacon of guidance, a testament to excellence, and a catalyst for achievement. Crafted with meticulous care and expertise, MathFlare Workbooks stand as paragons of educational excellence, designed to nurture young minds, ignite a passion for learning, and develop a deep-rooted understanding of mathematical concepts.

Picture this: your child eagerly delves into the pages of Mathflare Workbook, greeted by a step-by-step guide illuminated with vivid examples that demystify complex mathematical concepts. With each turn of the page, they embark on a journey of discovery, encountering thoughtfully curated practice questions that reinforce learning and hone problem-solving skills. And when they unveil the answers to those very questions, a sense of accomplishment blossoms within them – a tangible reward for their hard work and dedication.

But MathFlare Workbooks are more than just tools for learning; they are pathways to comprehension, fostering a deep-seated understanding of mathematical concepts through a sequential, logical flow. From fundamental principles to advanced problem-solving strategies, every chapter builds upon the last, ensuring a robust foundation upon which future knowledge can be constructed.

As parents, we yearn for nothing more than to see our children thrive, to witness the spark of inspiration ignited within them as they conquer academic challenges with confidence and poise. MathFlare Workbooks serve as partners in this noble endeavor, offering not just practice questions, but the keys to unlocking a world of opportunity.

And for teachers, MathFlare Workbooks stand as invaluable allies in the quest to cultivate mathematical proficiency in the classroom. With answers readily available, instructors can focus on guiding and nurturing their students, confident in the knowledge that MathFlare Workbooks provide a solid framework upon which to build.

In the pages of MathFlare Workbooks, we find not just the promise of academic excellence, but the seeds of a brighter tomorrow. So let us embrace the power of mathematics, let us champion the journey of learning, and let us pave the way for a generation of young minds poised to shape the world. With MathFlare Workbooks as our guide, the possibilities are infinite, and the future, bright.

Table of Contents

MathFlare
MATH WORKBOOK
Grade 2
Step by Step Guide and Essential Practice with Answers
Addition Subtraction
Multiplication
Place Value and Expanded Notations
Geometry
MathFlare Publishing

MathFlare
MATH WORKBOOK
Grade 2-3
Step by Step Guide and Essential Practice with Answers
Addition Subtraction
Multiplication and Division
Place Value and Expanded Notations
Geometry
MathFlare Publishing

MathFlare
MATH WORKBOOK
Grade 3
Step by Step Guide and Essential Practice with Answers
Multiplication and Division
Decimals
Place Value and Expanded Notations
Fractions and Geometry
MathFlare Publishing

MathFlare
MATH WORKBOOK
Grade 1
Step by Step Guide and Essential Practice with Answers
Counting and Numbers
Addition and Subtraction
Place Value and Expanded Notations
Understanding Time
MathFlare Publishing

MathFlare
MATH WORKBOOK
Grade 1-2
Step by Step Guide and Essential Practice with Answers
Counting and Numbers
Addition and Subtraction
Place Value and Expanded Notations
Understanding Time
MathFlare Publishing

MathFlare
MATH WORKBOOK
Grade 3-4
Step by Step Guide and Essential Practice with Answers
Addition Subtraction
Multiplication Division
Place Value and Expanded Notations
Fractions and Geometry
MathFlare Publishing

MathFlare
MATH WORKBOOK
Grade 4
Step by Step Guide and Essential Practice with Answers
Addition Subtraction
Multiplication Division
Place Value and Expanded Notations
Fractions and Geometry
MathFlare Publishing

MathFlare
MATH WORKBOOK
Grade 4-5
Step by Step Guide and Essential Practice with Answers
Multiplication Division
Place Value and Expanded Notations
Fractions and Geometry
Unit Conversion
MathFlare Publishing

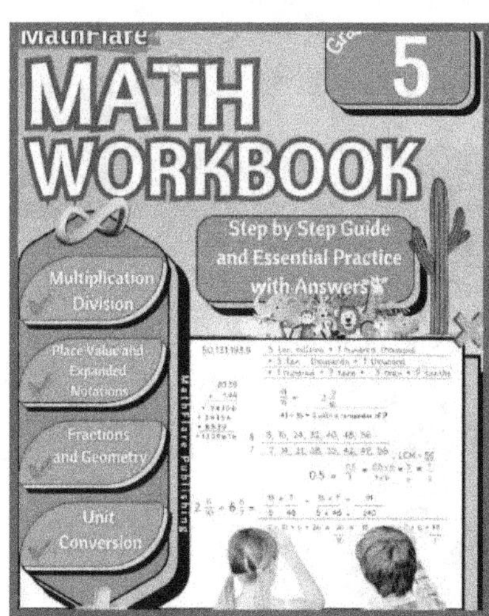
MathFlare
Grade 5
MATH WORKBOOK
Step by Step Guide and Essential Practice with Answers
Multiplication Division
Place Value and Expanded Notations
Fractions and Geometry
Unit Conversion
MathFlare Publishing

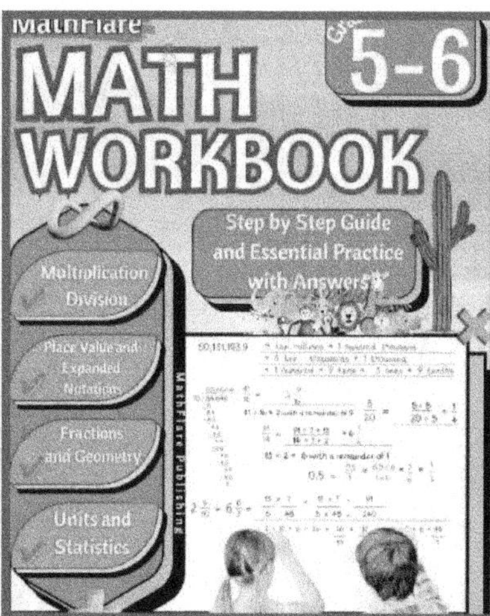
MathFlare
Grade 5-6
MATH WORKBOOK
Step by Step Guide and Essential Practice with Answers
Multiplication Division
Place Value and Expanded Notations
Fractions and Geometry
Units and Statistics
MathFlare Publishing

MathFlare
Grade 6
MATH WORKBOOK
Step by Step Guide and Essential Practice with Answers
Integers and Statistics
Arithmetic and Pre-Algebra
Fractions and Geometry
Ratio and Percentage
MathFlare Publishing

MathFlare
Grade 6-7
MATH WORKBOOK
Step by Step Guide and Essential Practice with Answers
Arithmetic and Pre-Algebra
Ratio, Percent Proportion
Geometry
Statistics
MathFlare Publishing

MathFlare
Grade 7
MATH WORKBOOK
Step by Step Guide and Essential Practice with Answers
Pre-Algebra
Ratio, Percent Proportion
Geometry
Statistics
MathFlare Publishing

MathFlare
Grade 7-8
MATH WORKBOOK
Step by Step Guide and Essential Practice with Answers
Pre-Algebra
Ratio, Percent Proportion
Geometry and Cartesian Plane
Statistics
MathFlare Publishing

MathFlare
Grade 8-9
MATH WORKBOOK
Step by Step Guide and Essential Practice with Answers
Pre-Algebra
Ratio, Proportion and Percentage
Linear Equations
Geometry and Cartesian Plane
MathFlare Publishing

MathFlare
Grade 8
MATH WORKBOOK
Step by Step Guide and Essential Practice with Answers
Pre-Algebra
Percentage
Linear Equations
Geometry
MathFlare Publishing

Multiplication

Multiplication

Multiplication is an easy way of adding numbers together quickly. Instead of adding the same number repeatedly, we use multiplication to find the total much faster.

For instance, rather than adding 2 + 2 + 2 + 2 + 2, we can multiply 2 by 5 to get the same result: 2 x 5 = 10.

Here, the first number (2) is called the multiplicand, second number (5) is the multiplier. The answer we get, in this case, 10, is called the product.

Let's think of multiplication as repeated addition.

Take 2 x 5, for example. It means adding 2 together five times, which we can illustrate as: 2 + 2 + 2 + 2 + 2 = 10

Multiplication can also be visualized as groups of objects. Imagine we have 2 groups, each containing 5 oranges.

To find the total number of oranges, we multiply the number of groups (2) by the number of oranges in each group (5):

2 groups of 5 oranges = 10 oranges

Expressed as multiplication: 2 x 5 = 10

In summary, multiplication offers various ways to approach it: through repeated addition or by envisioning groups of objects. It's a powerful tool that makes solving math problems much quicker and more efficient!

We can also use the following table to quickly remember multiplication facts. The intersection of two points shows the product of two numbers.

For instance, the product of 5 x 6 = 30, or 6 x 5 = 30.

	1	2	3	4	5	6	7	8	9	10
1	1	2	3	4	5	6	7	8	9	10
2	2	4	6	8	10	12	14	16	18	20
3	3	6	9	12	15	18	21	24	27	30
4	4	8	12	16	20	24	28	32	36	40
5	5	10	15	20	25	30	35	40	45	50
6	6	12	18	24	30	36	42	48	54	60
7	7	14	21	28	35	42	49	56	63	70
8	8	16	24	32	40	48	56	64	72	80
9	9	18	27	36	45	54	63	72	81	90
10	10	20	30	40	50	60	70	80	90	100

Commutative Property of Multiplication

The commutative property of multiplication is a special rule in math that tells us the order of the numbers being multiplied doesn't affect the result.

For instance, let's take 2 x 5. If we switch the order of the numbers, multiplying 5 by 2 instead, we'll still end up with the same answer: 2 x 5 = 10, or 5 x 2 = 10.

So, whether we multiply 2 by 5 or 5 by 2, we get 10. That's the commutative property of multiplication in action!

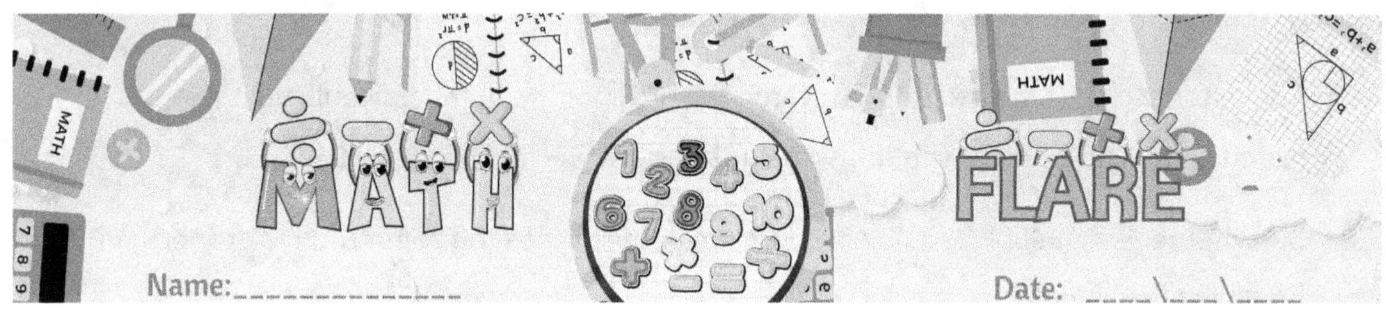

Multiplication by 1

1. 1
× 5

2. 1
× 2

3. 1
× 6

4. 4
× 1

5. 1
× 3

6. 7
× 1

7. 8
× 1

8. 1
× 9

9. 1
× 1

10. 2
× 1

11. 6
× 1

12. 3
× 1

13. 1
× 7

14. 5
× 1

15. 1
× 8

16. 1
× 4

17. 9
× 1

18. 6
× 1

19. 4
× 1

20. 1
× 1

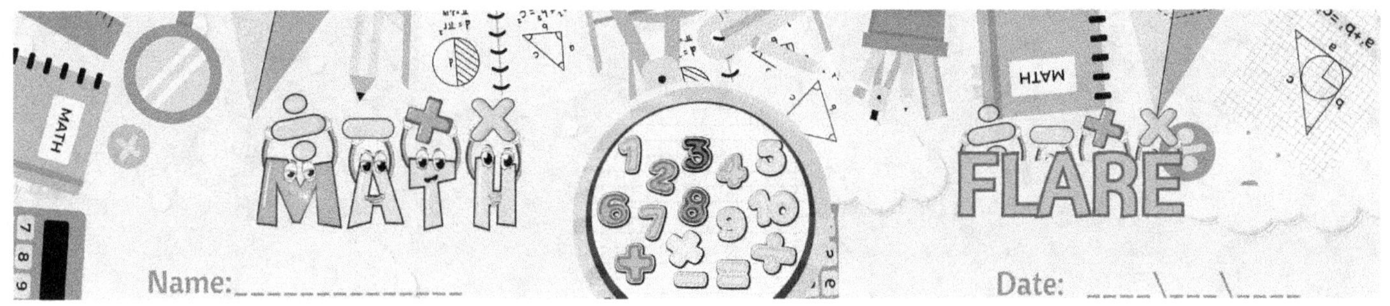

Multiplication by 2

21. 4
   × 2

22. 2
   × 8

23. 2
   × 6

24. 2
   × 3

25. 1
   × 2

26. 2
   × 2

27. 2
   × 5

28. 2
   × 9

29. 7
   × 2

30. 2
   × 1

31. 2
   × 4

32. 5
   × 2

33. 3
   × 2

34. 9
   × 2

35. 2
   × 7

36. 6
   × 2

37. 8
   × 2

38. 6
   × 2

39. 7
   × 2

40. 2
   × 8

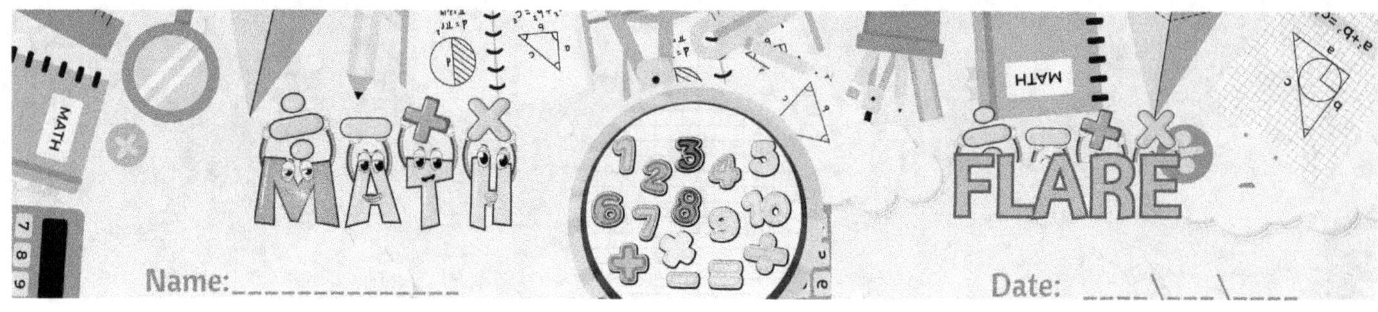

Multiplication by 3

41. 1 × 3

42. 6 × 3

43. 3 × 3

44. 3 × 7

45. 4 × 3

46. 2 × 3

47. 3 × 8

48. 3 × 5

49. 9 × 3

50. 8 × 3

51. 7 × 3

52. 3 × 1

53. 3 × 9

54. 5 × 3

55. 3 × 4

56. 3 × 2

57. 3 × 6

58. 8 × 3

59. 9 × 3

60. 8 × 3

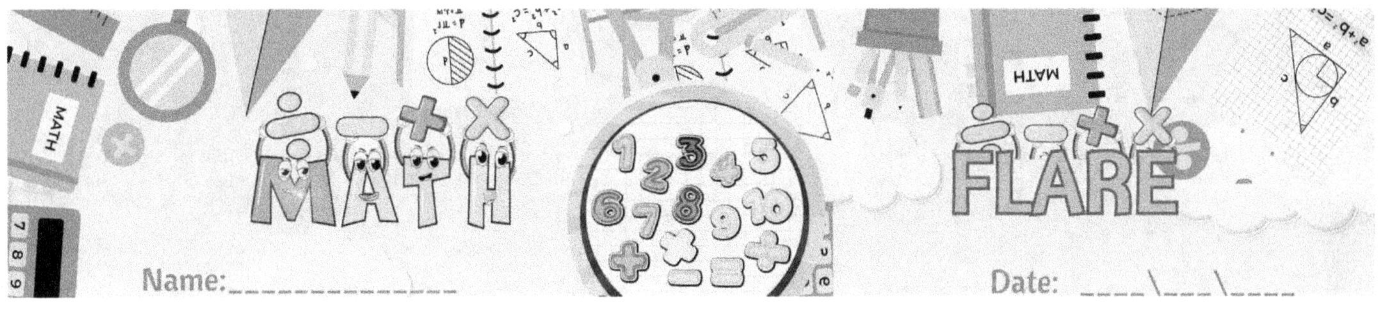

Multiplication by 4

61.   4
   × 3

62.   4
   × 4

63.   4
   × 5

64.   7
   × 4

65.   4
   × 6

66.   1
   × 4

67.   8
   × 4

68.   4
   × 9

69.   4
   × 2

70.   6
   × 4

71.   5
   × 4

72.   4
   × 7

73.   3
   × 4

74.   4
   × 8

75.   9
   × 4

76.   2
   × 4

77.   4
   × 1

78.   4
   × 9

79.   4
   × 4

80.   4
   × 2

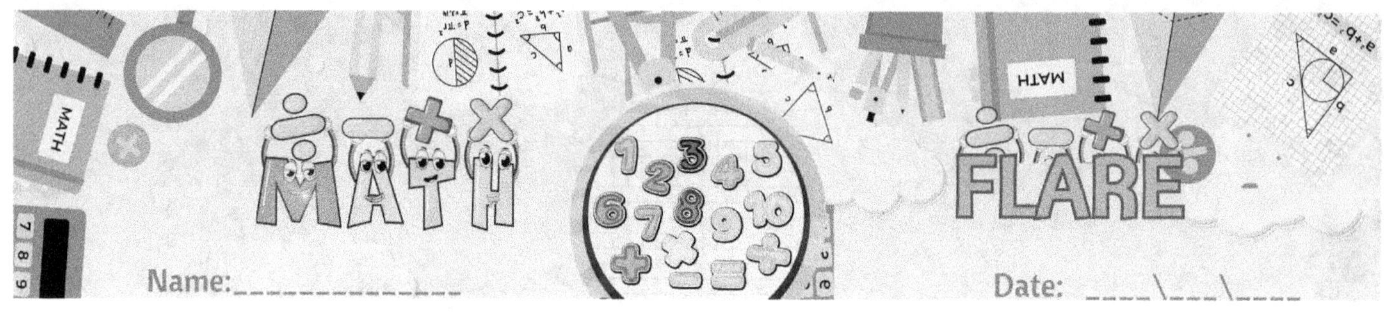

Multiplication by 5

81.
$$\begin{array}{r} 5 \\ \times\ 5 \\ \hline \end{array}$$

82.
$$\begin{array}{r} 2 \\ \times\ 5 \\ \hline \end{array}$$

83.
$$\begin{array}{r} 5 \\ \times\ 3 \\ \hline \end{array}$$

84.
$$\begin{array}{r} 5 \\ \times\ 4 \\ \hline \end{array}$$

85.
$$\begin{array}{r} 5 \\ \times\ 8 \\ \hline \end{array}$$

86.
$$\begin{array}{r} 5 \\ \times\ 9 \\ \hline \end{array}$$

87.
$$\begin{array}{r} 5 \\ \times\ 7 \\ \hline \end{array}$$

88.
$$\begin{array}{r} 5 \\ \times\ 1 \\ \hline \end{array}$$

89.
$$\begin{array}{r} 5 \\ \times\ 6 \\ \hline \end{array}$$

90.
$$\begin{array}{r} 8 \\ \times\ 5 \\ \hline \end{array}$$

91.
$$\begin{array}{r} 3 \\ \times\ 5 \\ \hline \end{array}$$

92.
$$\begin{array}{r} 9 \\ \times\ 5 \\ \hline \end{array}$$

93.
$$\begin{array}{r} 4 \\ \times\ 5 \\ \hline \end{array}$$

94.
$$\begin{array}{r} 5 \\ \times\ 2 \\ \hline \end{array}$$

95.
$$\begin{array}{r} 6 \\ \times\ 5 \\ \hline \end{array}$$

96.
$$\begin{array}{r} 7 \\ \times\ 5 \\ \hline \end{array}$$

97.
$$\begin{array}{r} 1 \\ \times\ 5 \\ \hline \end{array}$$

98.
$$\begin{array}{r} 7 \\ \times\ 5 \\ \hline \end{array}$$

99.
$$\begin{array}{r} 5 \\ \times\ 4 \\ \hline \end{array}$$

100.
$$\begin{array}{r} 7 \\ \times\ 5 \\ \hline \end{array}$$

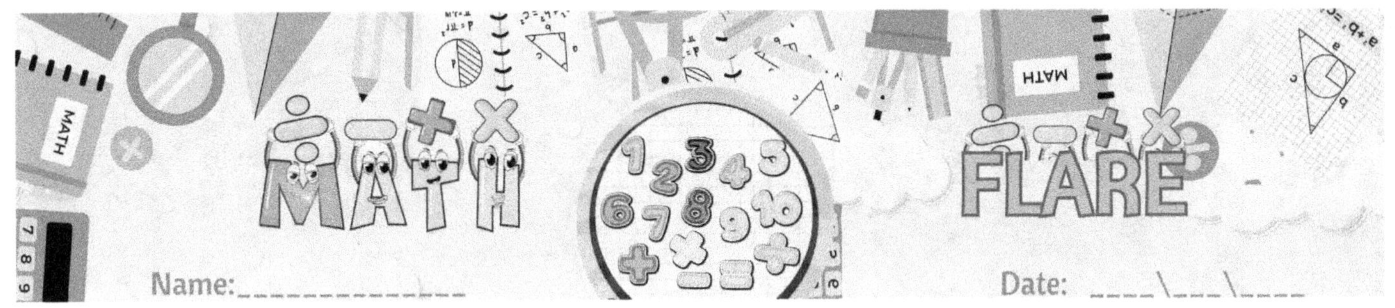

Multiplication by 6

101. 8
× 6

102. 3
× 6

103. 6
× 5

104. 7
× 6

105. 2
× 6

106. 6
× 6

107. 1
× 6

108. 4
× 6

109. 9
× 6

110. 6
× 3

111. 6
× 9

112. 5
× 6

113. 6
× 7

114. 6
× 2

115. 6
× 8

116. 6
× 4

117. 6
× 1

118. 6
× 2

119. 6
× 1

120. 5
× 6

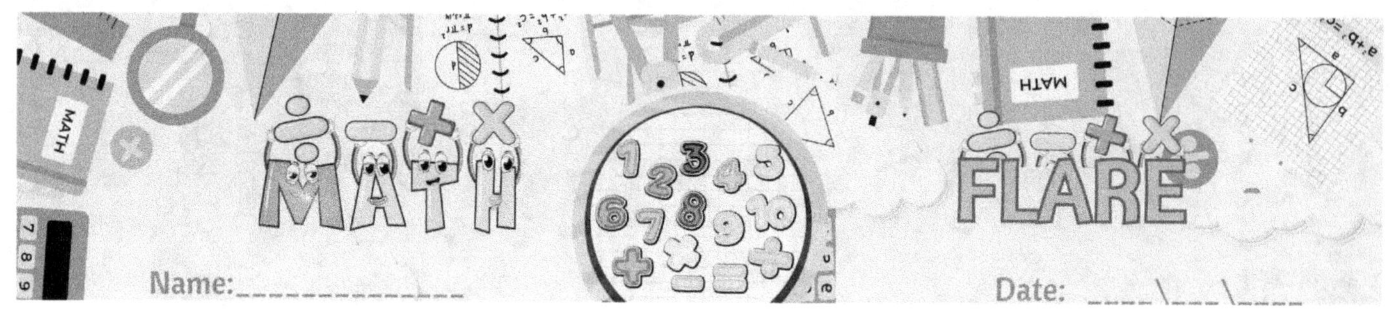

Multiplication by 7

121.   7
     × 8
_____

122.   7
     × 6
_____

123.   4
     × 7
_____

124.   7
     × 1
_____

125.   3
     × 7
_____

126.   5
     × 7
_____

127.   7
     × 7
_____

128.   7
     × 2
_____

129.   7
     × 9
_____

130.   7
     × 3
_____

131.   7
     × 4
_____

132.   9
     × 7
_____

133.   8
     × 7
_____

134.   6
     × 7
_____

135.   7
     × 5
_____

136.   2
     × 7
_____

137.   1
     × 7
_____

138.   7
     × 4
_____

139.   7
     × 7
_____

140.   2
     × 7
_____

Multiplication by 8

141.
8
× 7

142.
8
× 5

143.
8
× 3

144.
8
× 8

145.
2
× 8

146.
8
× 4

147.
1
× 8

148.
6
× 8

149.
8
× 9

150.
7
× 8

151.
5
× 8

152.
8
× 2

153.
9
× 8

154.
3
× 8

155.
4
× 8

156.
8
× 1

157.
8
× 6

158.
8
× 5

159.
8
× 9

160.
7
× 8

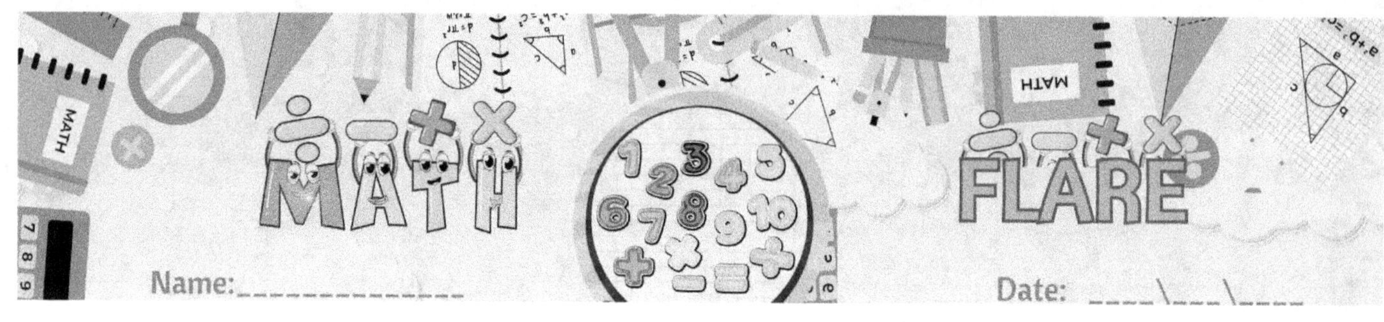

Multiplication by 9

161. 9 × 6	162. 9 × 4	163. 9 × 1	164. 7 × 9
165. 9 × 8	166. 9 × 5	167. 9 × 2	168. 3 × 9
169. 9 × 9	170. 9 × 7	171. 9 × 3	172. 8 × 9
173. 6 × 9	174. 1 × 9	175. 4 × 9	176. 2 × 9
177. 5 × 9	178. 9 × 3	179. 8 × 9	180. 9 × 2

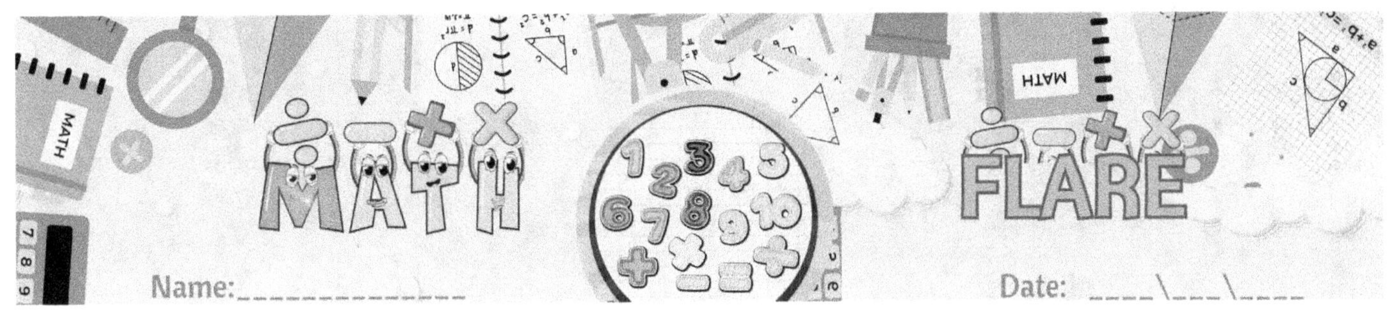

Multiplication by 10

181.   3
× 10

182.   4
× 10

183.   10
× 6

184.   8
× 10

185.   5
× 10

186.   1
× 10

187.   7
× 10

188.   10
× 2

189.   10
× 9

190.   2
× 10

191.   10
× 5

192.   10
× 3

193.   10
× 8

194.   6
× 10

195.   10
× 1

196.   10
× 7

197.   9
× 10

198.   10
× 4

199.   4
× 10

200.   10
× 4

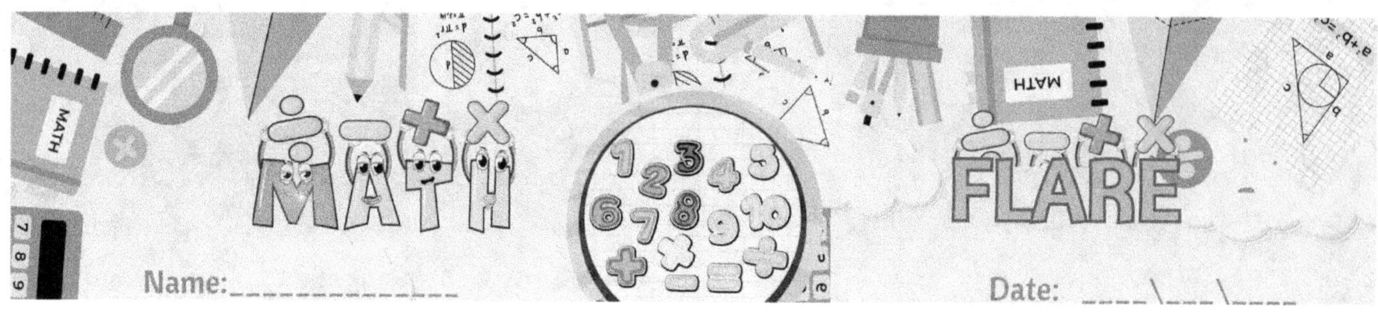

Basic Multiplication
Find the product.

201. 8
    × 2

202. 6
    × 8

203. 2
    × 2

204. 1
    × 5

205. 2
    × 3

206. 4
    × 5

207. 10
    × 5

208. 4
    × 7

209. 2
    × 4

210. 8
    × 6

211. 9
    × 3

212. 9
    × 5

213. 9
    × 4

214. 3
    × 7

215. 4
    × 6

216. 4
    × 3

217. 7
    × 9

218. 10
    × 8

219. 2
    × 5

220. 1
    × 6

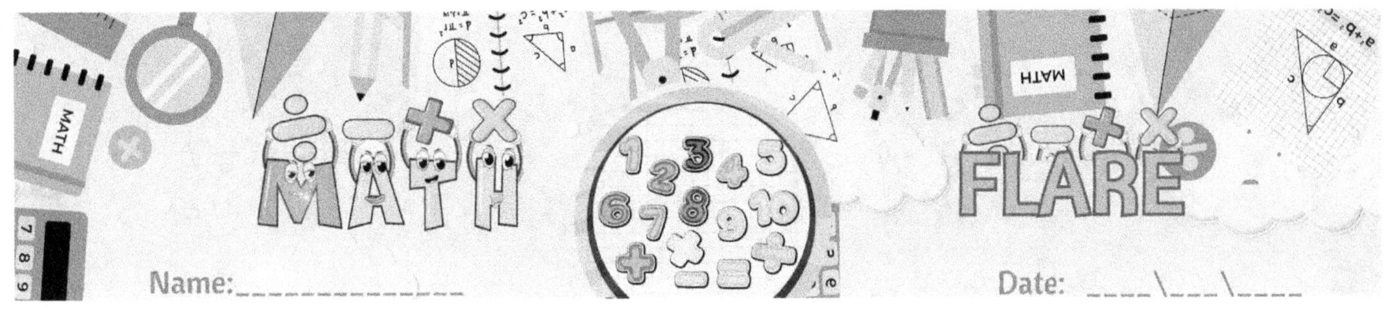

Name:____________________   Date: ____________

221. 10 × 9	222. 4 × 8	223. 8 × 10	224. 4 × 4
225. 9 × 7	226. 3 × 5	227. 5 × 1	228. 2 × 8
229. 8 × 5	230. 8 × 4	231. 3 × 4	232. 6 × 3
233. 3 × 10	234. 1 × 8	235. 5 × 10	236. 7 × 2
237. 1 × 4	238. 5 × 5	239. 3 × 6	240. 8 × 9

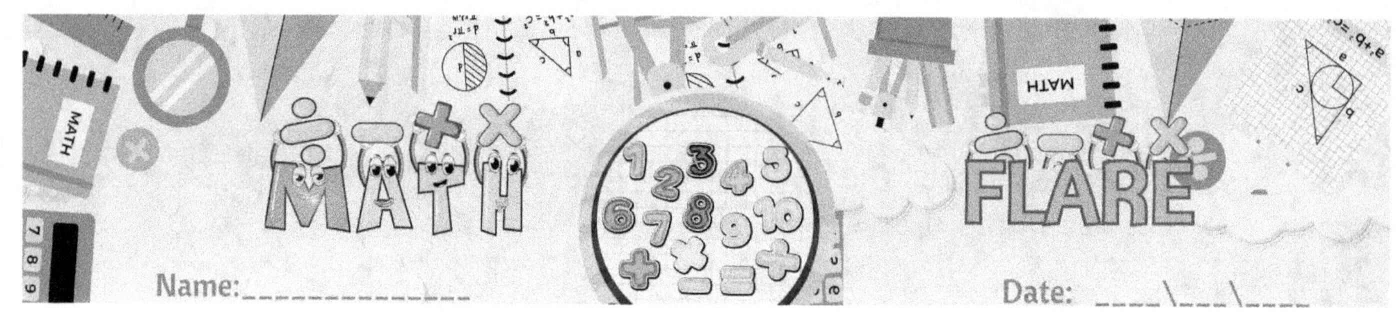

241. 7 × 1	242. 2 × 9	243. 8 × 7	244. 6 × 2
245. 9 × 8	246. 1 × 10	247. 1 × 3	248. 5 × 6
249. 1 × 1	250. 5 × 9	251. 8 × 1	252. 5 × 8
253. 3 × 2	254. 5 × 4	255. 5 × 7	256. 7 × 5
257. 6 × 7	258. 1 × 9	259. 5 × 2	260. 7 × 6

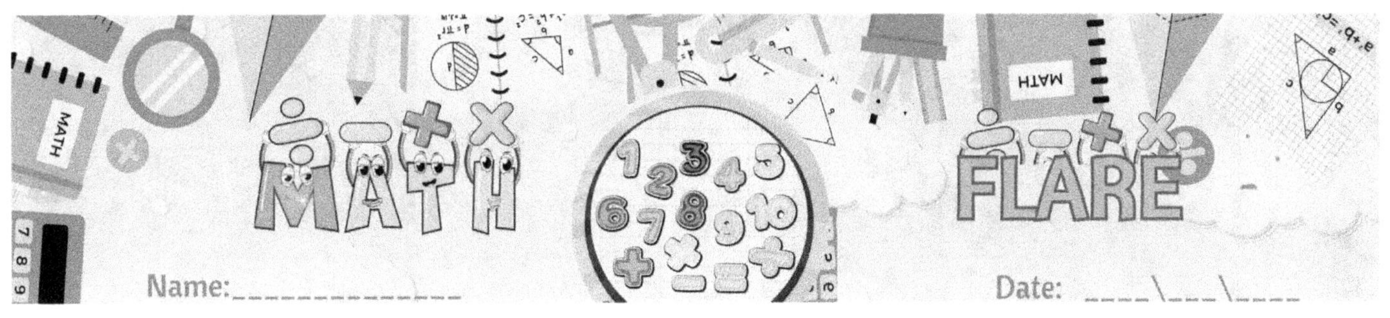

261. $\begin{array}{r} 2 \\ \times\ 7 \\ \hline \end{array}$	262. $\begin{array}{r} 5 \\ \times\ 3 \\ \hline \end{array}$	263. $\begin{array}{r} 4 \\ \times\ 1 \\ \hline \end{array}$	264. $\begin{array}{r} 6 \\ \times\ 9 \\ \hline \end{array}$
265. $\begin{array}{r} 6 \\ \times\ 6 \\ \hline \end{array}$	266. $\begin{array}{r} 3 \\ \times\ 3 \\ \hline \end{array}$	267. $\begin{array}{r} 1 \\ \times\ 7 \\ \hline \end{array}$	268. $\begin{array}{r} 4 \\ \times\ 10 \\ \hline \end{array}$
269. $\begin{array}{r} 10 \\ \times\ 3 \\ \hline \end{array}$	270. $\begin{array}{r} 4 \\ \times\ 2 \\ \hline \end{array}$	271. $\begin{array}{r} 2 \\ \times\ 6 \\ \hline \end{array}$	272. $\begin{array}{r} 9 \\ \times\ 6 \\ \hline \end{array}$
273. $\begin{array}{r} 6 \\ \times\ 5 \\ \hline \end{array}$	274. $\begin{array}{r} 7 \\ \times\ 7 \\ \hline \end{array}$	275. $\begin{array}{r} 9 \\ \times\ 2 \\ \hline \end{array}$	276. $\begin{array}{r} 7 \\ \times\ 4 \\ \hline \end{array}$
277. $\begin{array}{r} 10 \\ \times\ 1 \\ \hline \end{array}$	278. $\begin{array}{r} 6 \\ \times\ 4 \\ \hline \end{array}$	279. $\begin{array}{r} 9 \\ \times\ 10 \\ \hline \end{array}$	280. $\begin{array}{r} 1 \\ \times\ 8 \\ \hline \end{array}$

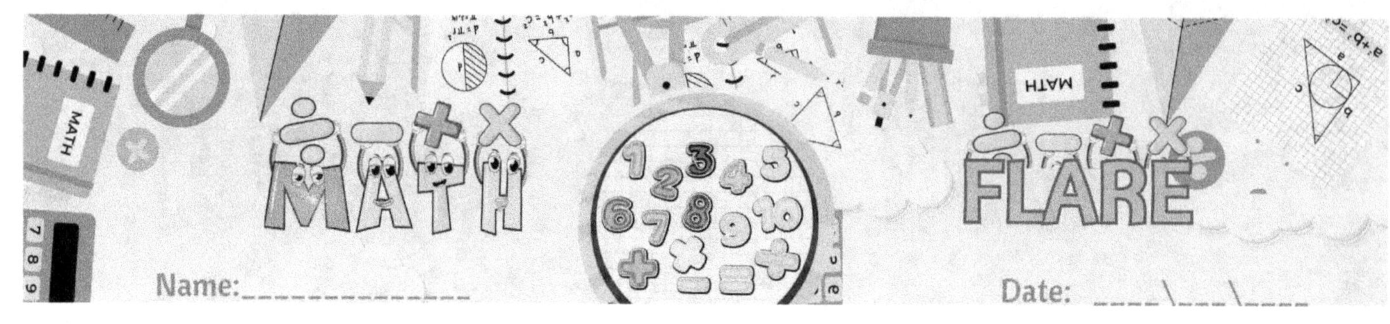

281. 9 × 9	282. 1 × 2	283. 8 × 8	284. 8 × 3
285. 4 × 9	286. 9 × 1	287. 3 × 9	288. 10 × 10
289. 2 × 10	290. 10 × 6	291. 2 × 1	292. 10 × 7
293. 3 × 8	294. 6 × 10	295. 3 × 1	296. 6 × 1
297. 10 × 2	298. 7 × 3	299. 7 × 10	300. 10 × 4

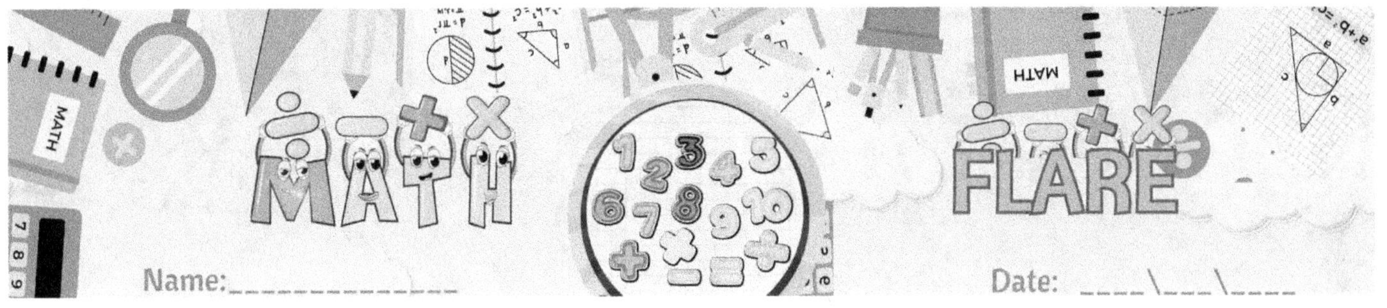

Basic Multiplication
Find the product.

301. 10 × 8 =

302. 7 × 7 =

303. 6 × 9 =

304. 5 × 8 =

305. 6 × 4 =

306. 9 × 2 =

307. 5 × 1 =

308. 4 × 3 =

309. 6 × 8 =

310. 5 × 3 =

311. 8 × 2 =

312. 2 × 3 =

313. 3 × 3 =

314. 8 × 3 =

315. 9 × 5 =

316. 4 × 6 =

317. 10 × 6 =

318. 3 × 6 =

319. 9 × 6 =

320. 3 × 9 =

321. 2 × 7 =

322. 7 × 5 =

323. 4 × 4 =

324. 1 × 2 =

325. 8 × 4 =

326. 2 × 9 =

327. 5 × 4 =

Name:_______________ Date: ____________

328. $2 \times 4 =$	329. $3 \times 2 =$	330. $4 \times 10 =$
331. $9 \times 3 =$	332. $8 \times 6 =$	333. $6 \times 10 =$
334. $6 \times 7 =$	335. $5 \times 7 =$	336. $8 \times 8 =$
337. $10 \times 1 =$	338. $2 \times 2 =$	339. $9 \times 4 =$
340. $2 \times 8 =$	341. $7 \times 9 =$	342. $6 \times 6 =$
343. $1 \times 3 =$	344. $8 \times 7 =$	345. $6 \times 5 =$
346. $7 \times 6 =$	347. $1 \times 6 =$	348. $5 \times 5 =$
349. $7 \times 8 =$	350. $1 \times 7 =$	351. $4 \times 5 =$
352. $5 \times 9 =$	353. $3 \times 5 =$	354. $1 \times 10 =$
355. $5 \times 2 =$	356. $3 \times 8 =$	357. $3 \times 4 =$
358. $2 \times 5 =$	359. $4 \times 7 =$	360. $6 \times 2 =$

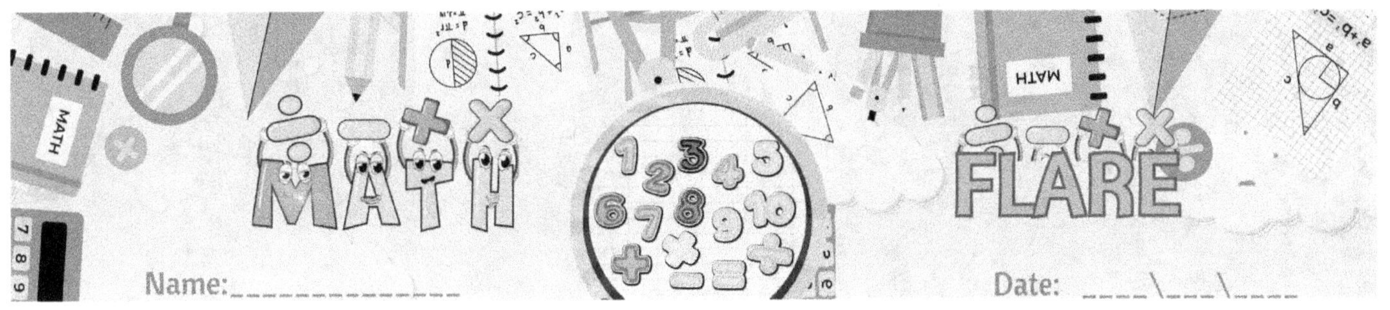

Name:_______________   Date: _______________

361. 9 × 9 =

362. 8 × 5 =

363. 6 × 3 =

364. 4 × 8 =

365. 9 × 10 =

366. 1 × 5 =

367. 1 × 8 =

368. 10 × 9 =

369. 4 × 1 =

370. 5 × 10 =

371. 8 × 1 =

372. 4 × 2 =

373. 7 × 3 =

374. 3 × 7 =

375. 1 × 4 =

376. 9 × 1 =

377. 2 × 1 =

378. 9 × 7 =

379. 3 × 10 =

380. 7 × 10 =

381. 7 × 4 =

382. 8 × 9 =

383. 6 × 1 =

384. 10 × 4 =

385. 10 × 7 =

386. 8 × 10 =

387. 10 × 2 =

388. 5 × 6 =

389. 2 × 6 =

390. 10 × 5 =

391. 10 × 3 =

392. 4 × 9 =

393. 7 × 2 =

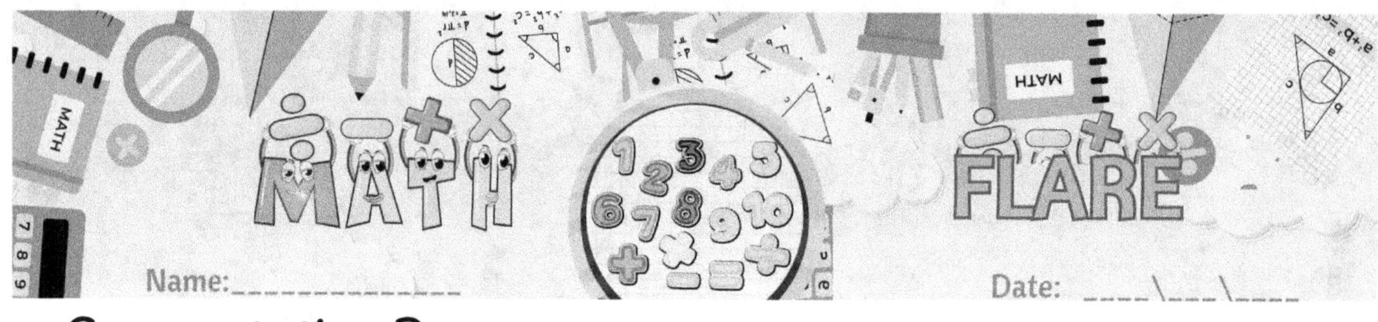

Commutative Property

Use the commutative property to fill the missing values.

394. $8 \times 2 = 2 \times \underline{}$

395. $7 \times 8 = 8 \times \underline{}$

396. $1 \times 6 = \underline{} \times 1$

397. $7 \times \underline{} = 5 \times 7$

398. $4 \times \underline{} = 5 \times 4$

399. $3 \times 9 = 9 \times \underline{}$

400. $9 \times \underline{} = 5 \times 9$

401. $3 \times 6 = \underline{} \times 3$

402. $3 \times 8 = \underline{} \times 3$

403. $10 \times 5 = \underline{} \times 10$

404. $3 \times 7 = 7 \times \underline{}$

405. $6 \times \underline{} = 5 \times 6$

406. $9 \times \underline{} = 2 \times 9$

407. $5 \times \underline{} = 7 \times 5$

408. $4 \times 6 = \underline{} \times 4$

409. $4 \times 7 = \underline{} \times 4$

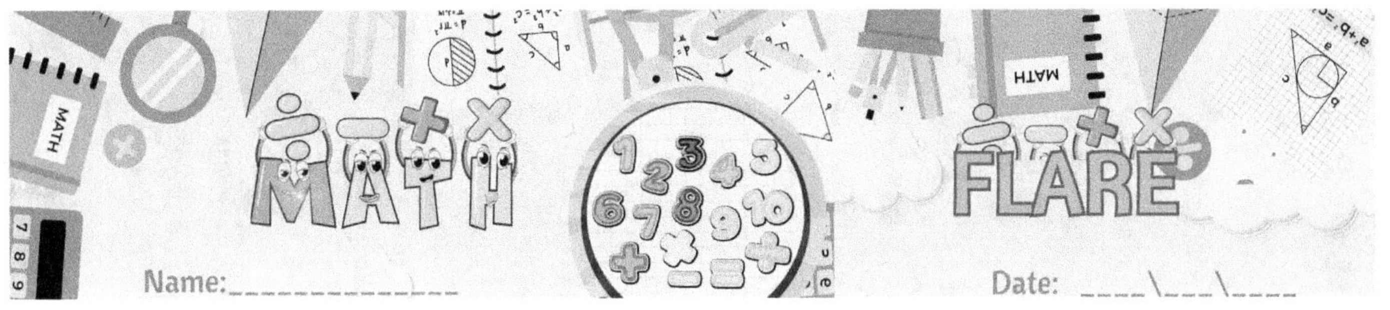

410. 9 × __ = 3 × 9

411. 3 × 10 = __ × 3

412. 6 × 2 = __ × 6

413. 5 × __ = 1 × 5

414. 2 × 7 = 7 × __

415. __ × 9 = 9 × 2

416. 9 × 1 = __ × 9

417. __ × 3 = 3 × 6

418. 5 × 9 = __ × 5

419. 5 × __ = 2 × 5

420. 4 × 9 = __ × 4

421. __ × 4 = 4 × 2

422. 2 × 8 = 8 × __

423. 8 × __ = 5 × 8

424. 5 × __ = 6 × 5

425. 1 × 9 = __ × 1

426. 1 × __ = 7 × 1

427. 7 × __ = 3 × 7

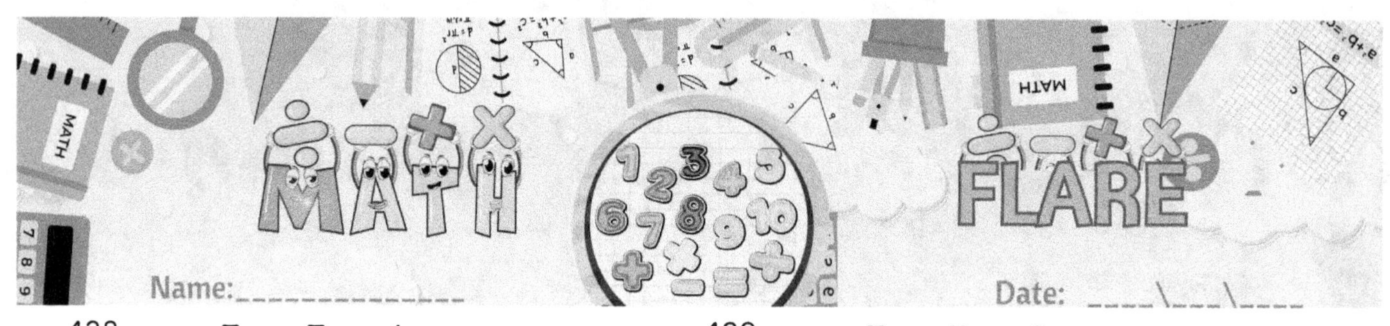

428. __ × 3 = 3 × 1

429. __ × 7 = 7 × 9

430. __ × 5 = 5 × 1

431. 8 × 3 = __ × 8

432. __ × 9 = 9 × 10

433. __ × 6 = 6 × 8

434. 7 × 1 = __ × 7

435. 1 × 8 = __ × 1

436. 3 × 4 = 4 × __

437. 9 × __ = 6 × 9

438. 3 × 2 = 2 × __

439. 10 × 4 = __ × 10

440. 6 × 9 = 9 × __

441. 8 × 1 = __ × 8

442. __ × 10 = 10 × 5

443. 2 × __ = 5 × 2

444. 7 × 10 = 10 × __

445. 7 × __ = 2 × 7

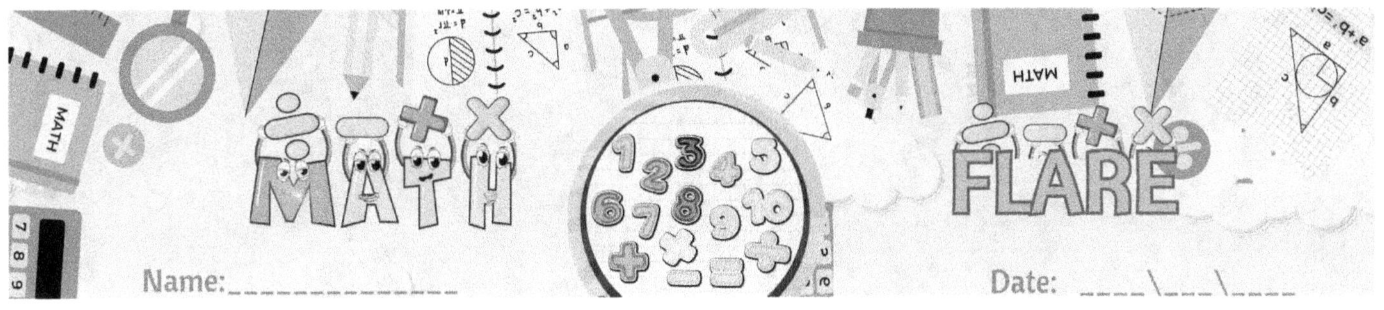

Matching the answers.

446.

a. 3 × 2 = _______ •	• J = 28
b. 2 × 3 = _______ •	• B = 6
c. 4 × 3 = _______ •	• C = 32
d. 4 × 8 = _______ •	• D = 32
e. 5 × 1 = _______ •	• H = 7
f. 1 × 6 = _______ •	• G = 6
g. 8 × 4 = _______ •	• I = 12
h. 4 × 7 = _______ •	• F = 6
i. 7 × 2 = _______ •	• E = 5
j. 1 × 7 = _______ •	• A = 14

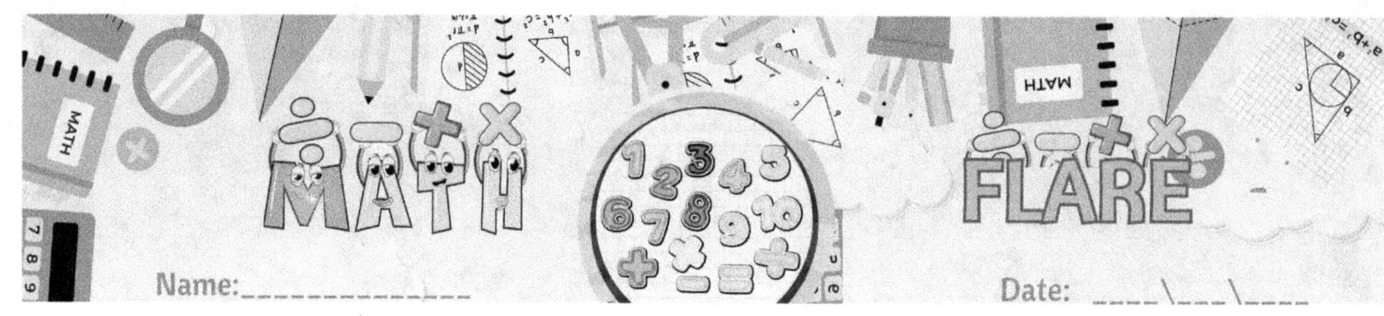

447.

a. 5 × 2 = _______ •	• I = 20
b. 8 × 9 = _______ •	• H = 35
c. 4 × 5 = _______ •	• E = 30
d. 2 × 8 = _______ •	• C = 10
e. 5 × 9 = _______ •	• G = 4
f. 6 × 5 = _______ •	• D = 16
g. 1 × 4 = _______ •	• B = 45
h. 10 × 10 = _____ •	• F = 48
i. 6 × 8 = _______ •	• A = 72
j. 5 × 7 = _______ •	• J = 100

448.

a. 4 × 3 = _______ •	• I = 20
b. 2 × 1 = _______ •	• H = 2
c. 10 × 3 = _______ •	• B = 9
d. 3 × 4 = _______ •	• C = 12
e. 3 × 3 = _______ •	• G = 12
f. 5 × 10 = _______ •	• J = 50
g. 9 × 1 = _______ •	• D = 72
h. 9 × 5 = _______ •	• A = 9
i. 10 × 2 = _______ •	• E = 45
j. 8 × 9 = _______ •	• F = 30

MathFlare - Multiplication 2nd Grade

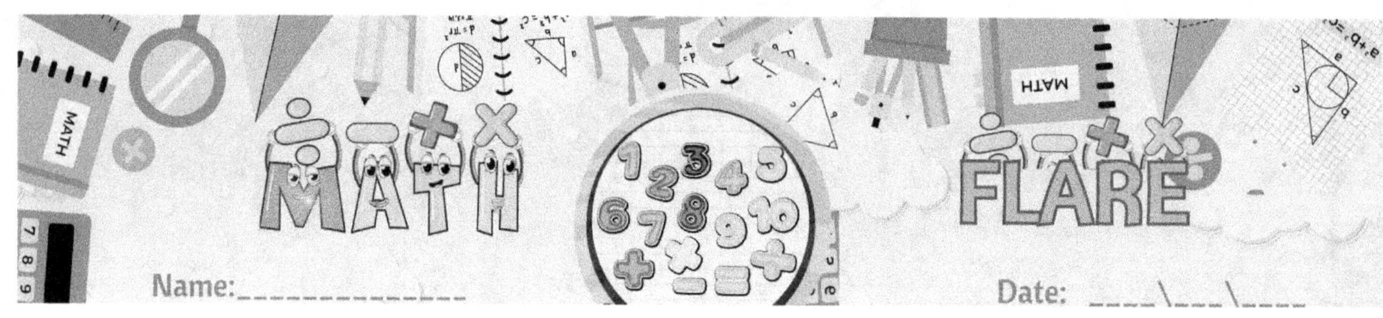

449.

a. 4 × 8 = _______ •	• H = 70
b. 3 × 3 = _______ •	• C = 72
c. 9 × 7 = _______ •	• F = 9
d. 8 × 9 = _______ •	• D = 42
e. 6 × 7 = _______ •	• A = 32
f. 6 × 2 = _______ •	• I = 63
g. 5 × 3 = _______ •	• B = 15
h. 8 × 4 = _______ •	• J = 12
i. 7 × 10 = _______ •	• E = 32
j. 7 × 6 = _______ •	• G = 42

MathFlare - Multiplication 2nd Grade

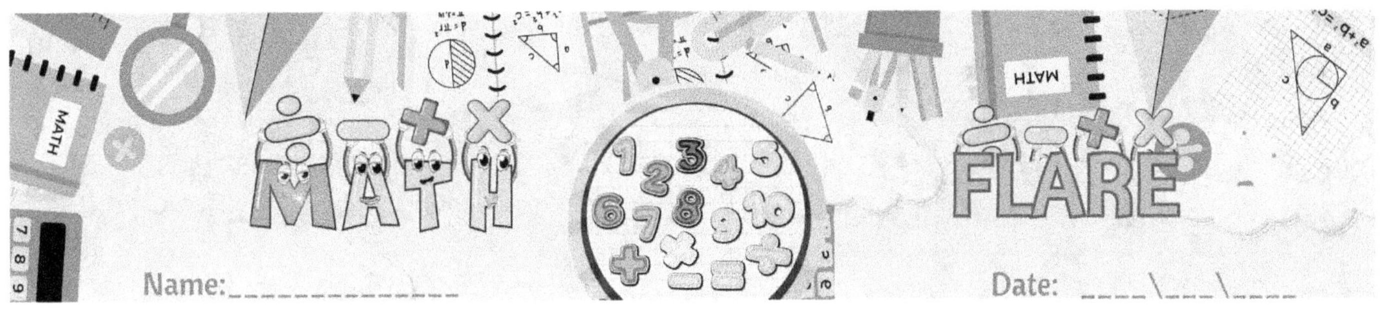

450.

a. 2 × 9 = _______   •

b. 5 × 3 = _______   •

c. 1 × 10 = _______   •

d. 5 × 5 = _______   •

e. 4 × 4 = _______   •

f. 6 × 5 = _______   •

g. 3 × 10 = _______   •

h. 2 × 5 = _______   •

i. 3 × 3 = _______   •

j. 1 × 1 = _______   •

• C = 30

• B = 1

• E = 10

• D = 25

• G = 16

• J = 15

• F = 9

• H = 30

• I = 10

• A = 18

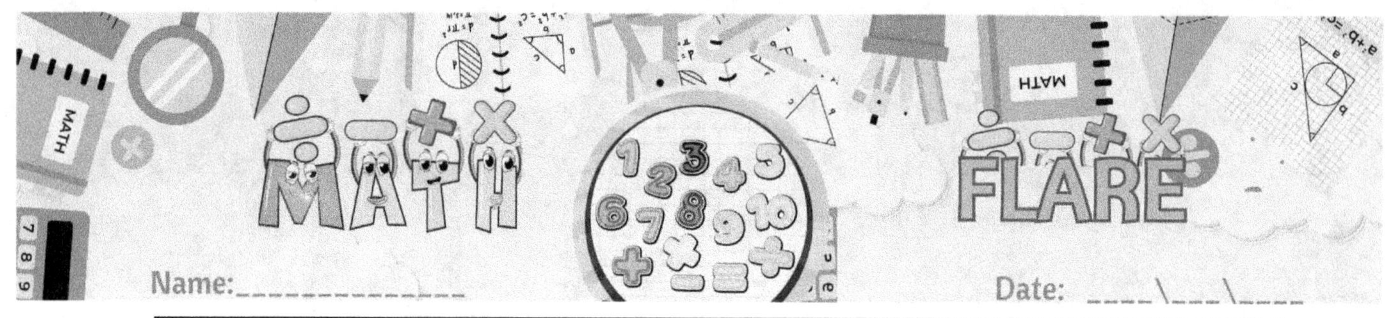

451.

a. 5 × 5 = _______   •   • A = 16

b. 3 × 1 = _______   •   • H = 25

c. 3 × 9 = _______   •   • B = 4

d. 2 × 1 = _______   •   • E = 56

e. 1 × 4 = _______   •   • G = 30

f. 8 × 2 = _______   •   • J = 8

g. 2 × 4 = _______   •   • F = 27

h. 3 × 10 = _______   •   • D = 2

i. 10 × 3 = _______   •   • I = 3

j. 7 × 8 = _______   •   • C = 30

452.

a. 9 × 5 = _______ •   • J = 14

b. 10 × 10 = _______ •   • G = 32

c. 1 × 3 = _______ •   • C = 50

d. 1 × 1 = _______ •   • D = 6

e. 6 × 1 = _______ •   • E = 3

f. 7 × 2 = _______ •   • I = 20

g. 10 × 5 = _______ •   • A = 45

h. 2 × 10 = _______ •   • H = 1

i. 8 × 4 = _______ •   • F = 100

j. 2 × 6 = _______ •   • B = 12

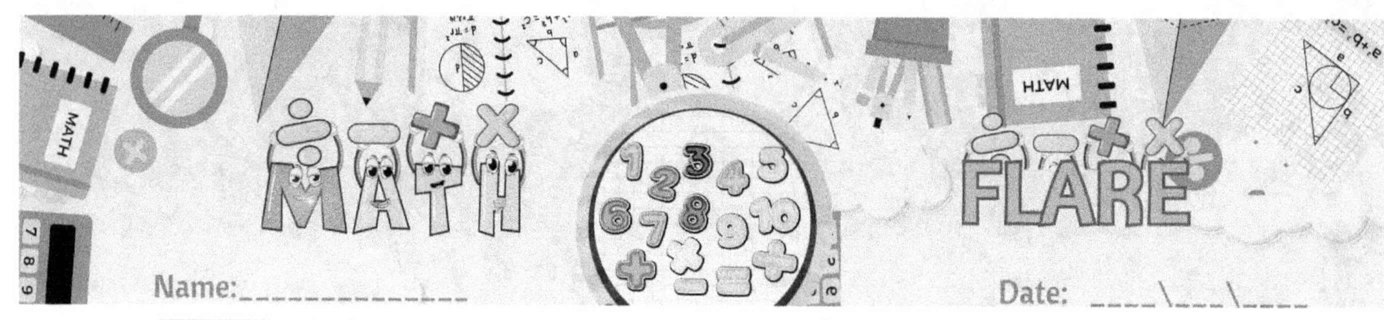

453.

a. 1 × 4 = ______ •	• J = 48
b. 5 × 2 = ______ •	• C = 40
c. 2 × 8 = ______ •	• A = 6
d. 1 × 2 = ______ •	• I = 56
e. 6 × 8 = ______ •	• B = 10
f. 2 × 3 = ______ •	• D = 24
g. 7 × 8 = ______ •	• E = 4
h. 5 × 8 = ______ •	• H = 15
i. 8 × 3 = ______ •	• G = 2
j. 5 × 3 = ______ •	• F = 16

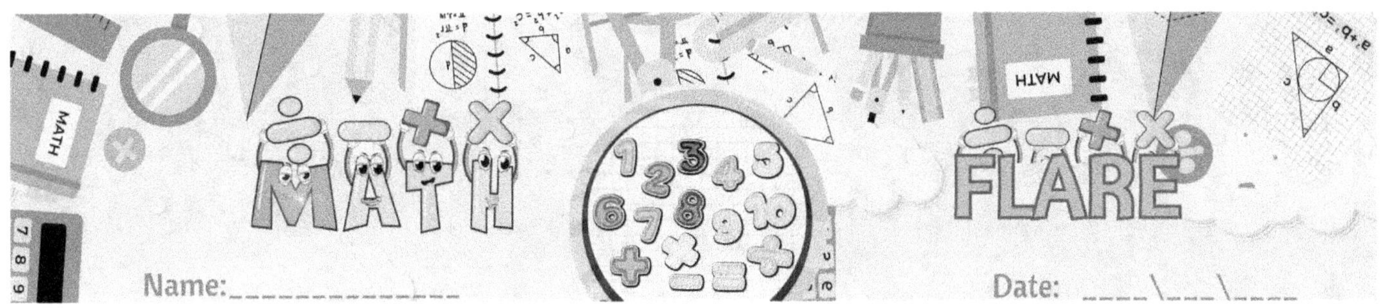

Name:_________________   Date: ______________

454.

a. 8 × 9 = _______ •

b. 1 × 5 = _______ •

c. 3 × 3 = _______ •

d. 7 × 9 = _______ •

e. 4 × 1 = _______ •

f. 3 × 2 = _______ •

g. 6 × 6 = _______ •

h. 7 × 6 = _______ •

i. 1 × 8 = _______ •

j. 8 × 7 = _______ •

• E = 36

• I = 5

• A = 9

• G = 56

• C = 8

• F = 4

• J = 42

• H = 72

• D = 6

• B = 63

455.

a. 10 × 4 = ______ •	• I = 27
b. 9 × 5 = ______ •	• B = 45
c. 2 × 9 = ______ •	• F = 18
d. 2 × 10 = ______ •	• G = 18
e. 8 × 2 = ______ •	• C = 40
f. 8 × 5 = ______ •	• D = 6
g. 3 × 9 = ______ •	• E = 16
h. 9 × 2 = ______ •	• J = 40
i. 7 × 5 = ______ •	• A = 20
j. 2 × 3 = ______ •	• H = 35

Multiplication Circles

456.

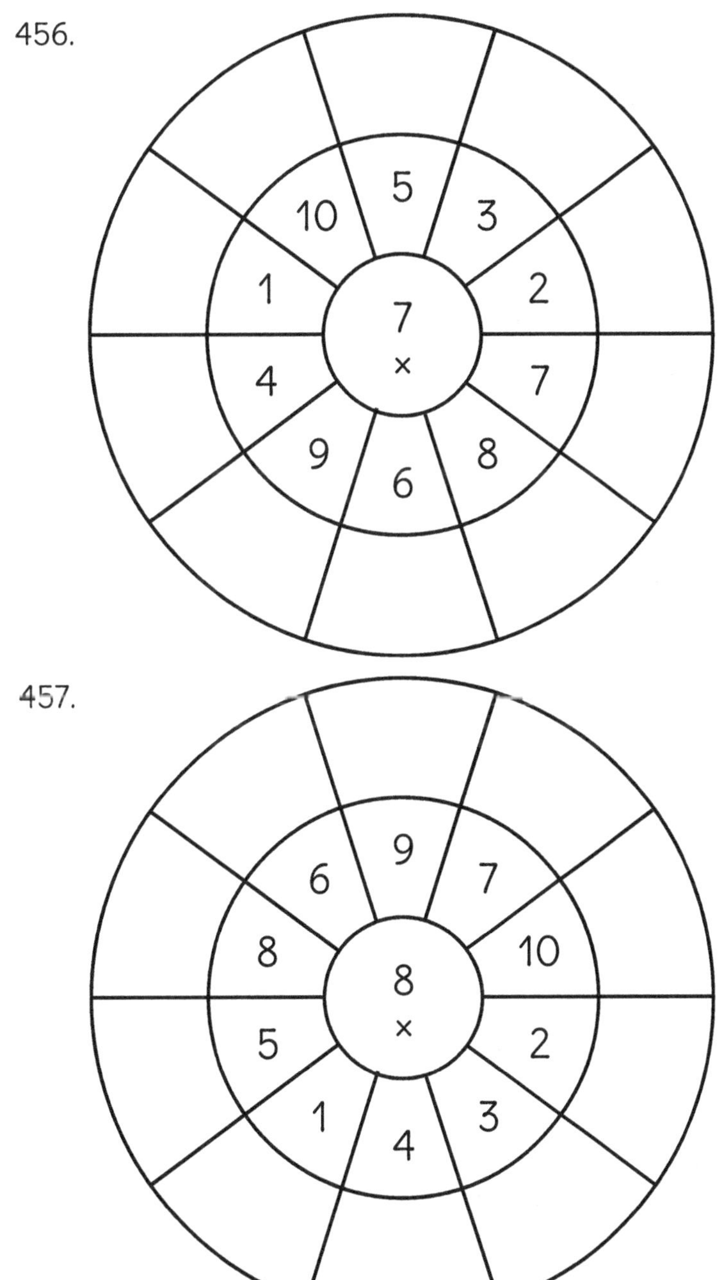

457.

458.

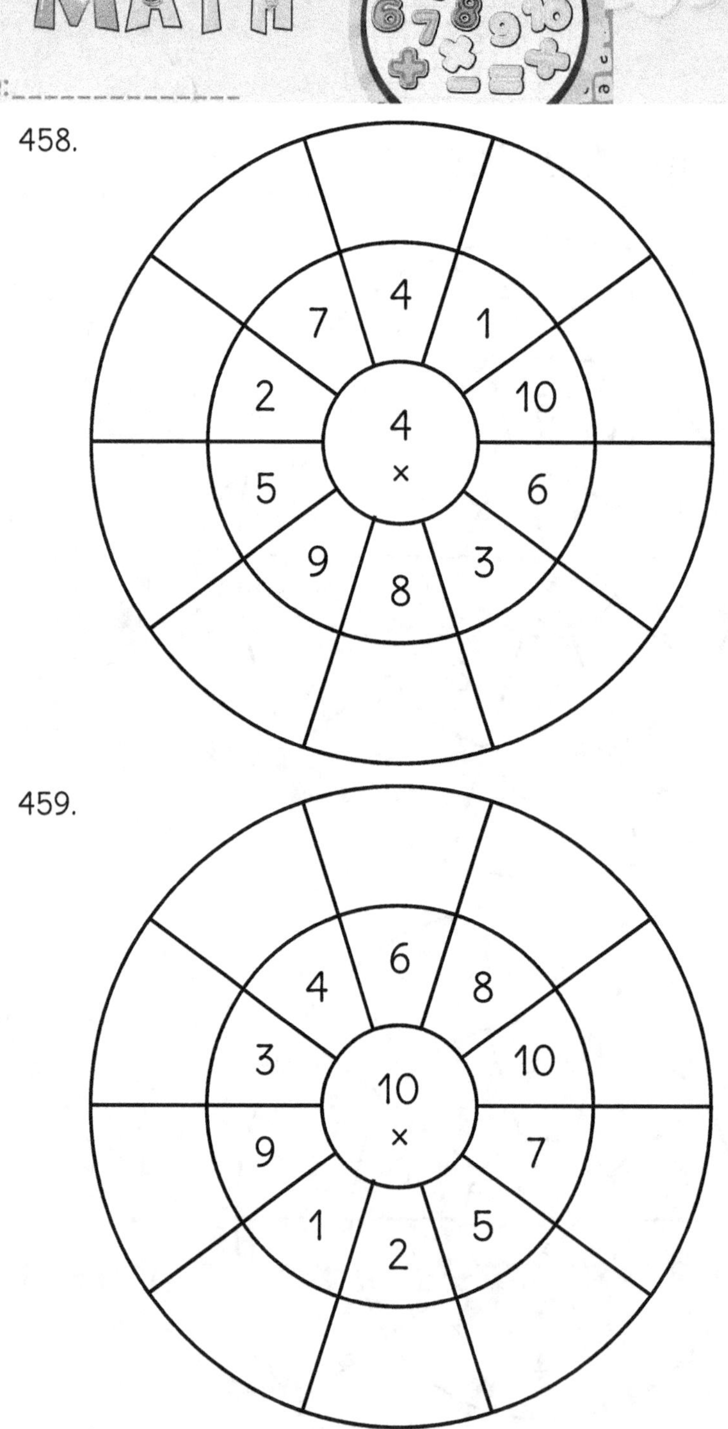

459.

460.

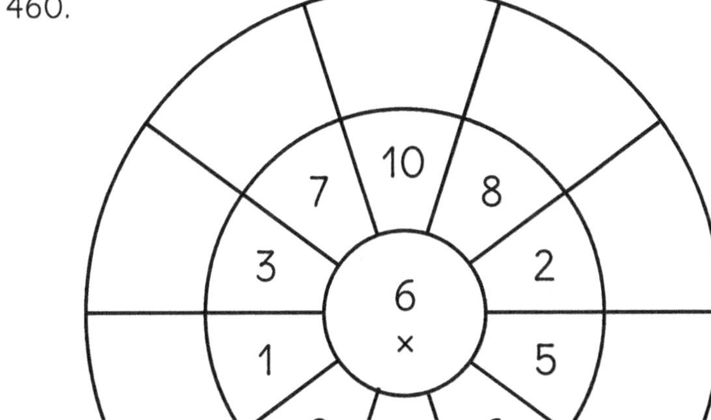

461.

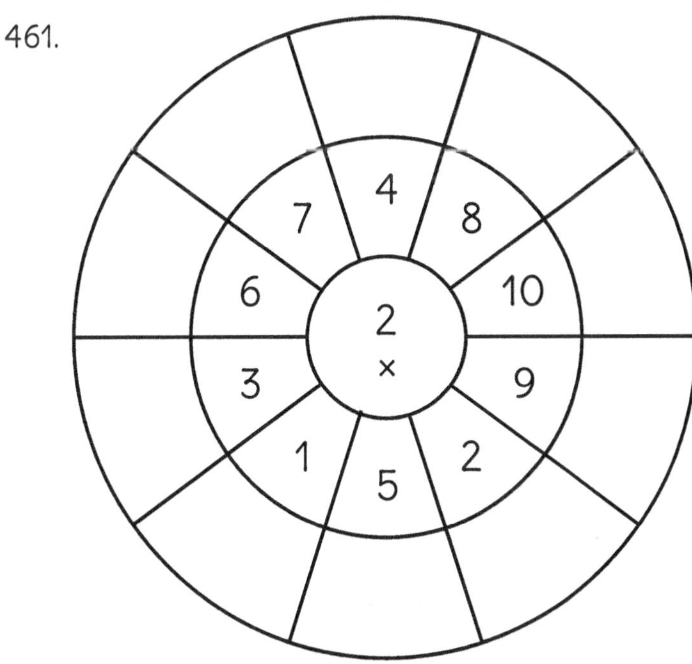

462.

463.

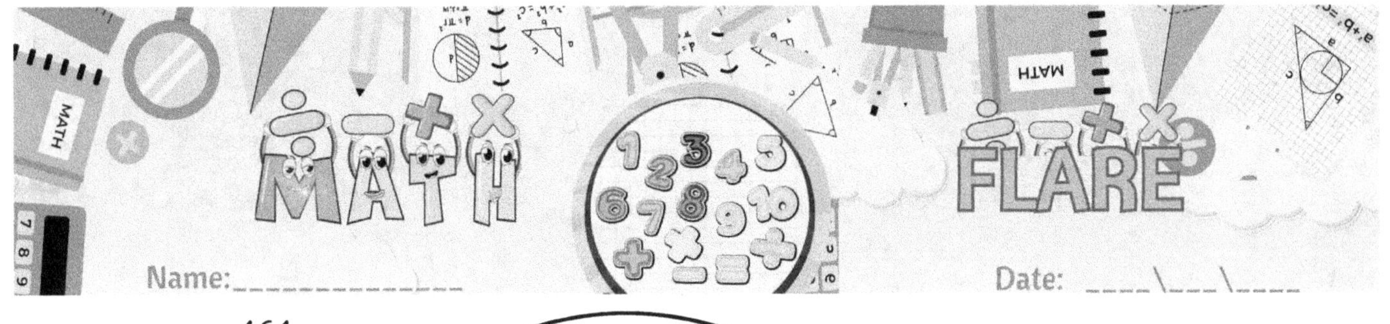

Name: _________________________ Date: ____ \ ____ \ ____

464.

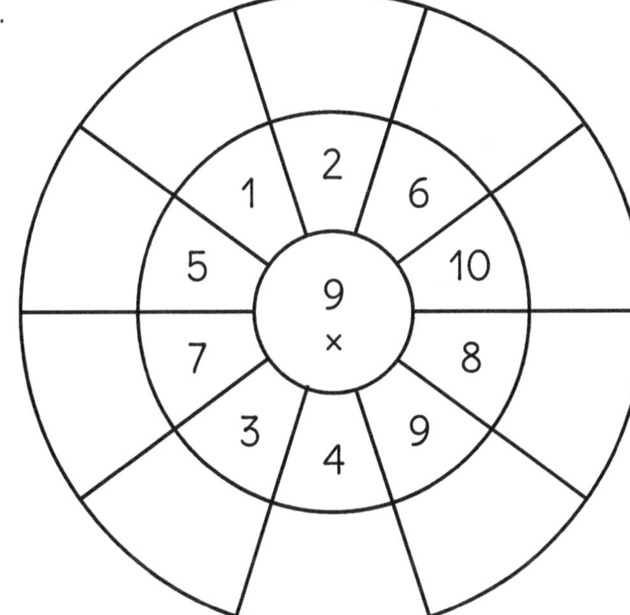

465.

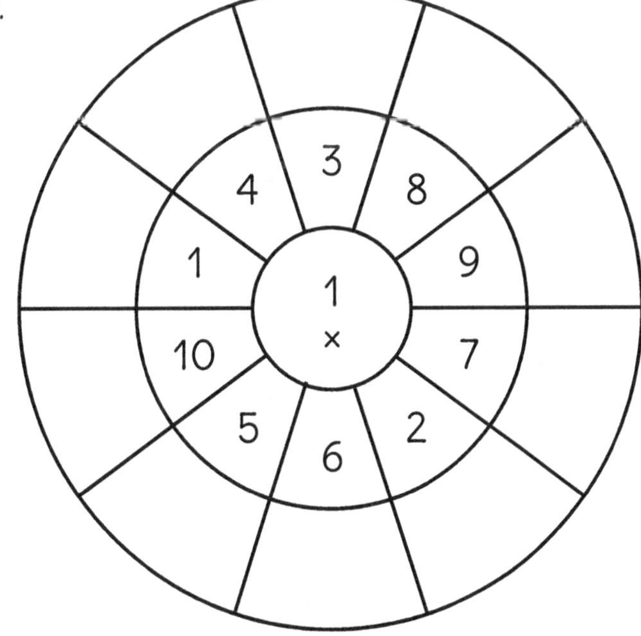

Complete the table.

466.

×	3	5	9	4	8	10	6	7	1	2
8	24			32						
7	21						42			
5	15				40	50			5	
1				4						2
4									4	
6	18			24						
3		15	27					21		
9										
2		10	18							
10			90							20

467.

×	1	2	6	5	9	4	7	8	3	10
1			6							
6			36	30			42			
4					36					
8	8									
10							70			
7				35	63					
2		4								
5			30					40	15	
9			54	45	81				27	
3				15	27		21			

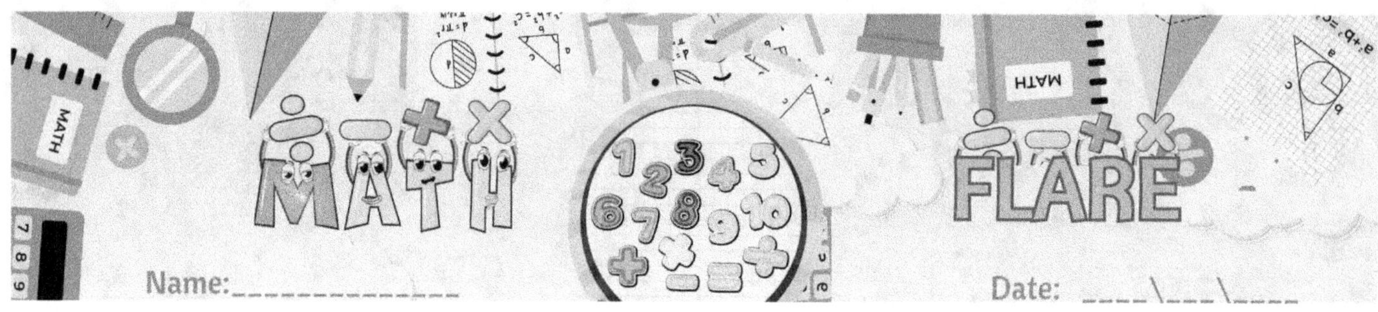

468.

×	6	4	8	1	7	2	5	3	9	10
5					35					
3			24			6				
6	36			6		12				
7				7					63	
9			72			18				90
2		8				4				
10					70	20		30		
1			8							
8					56			24		
4	24									

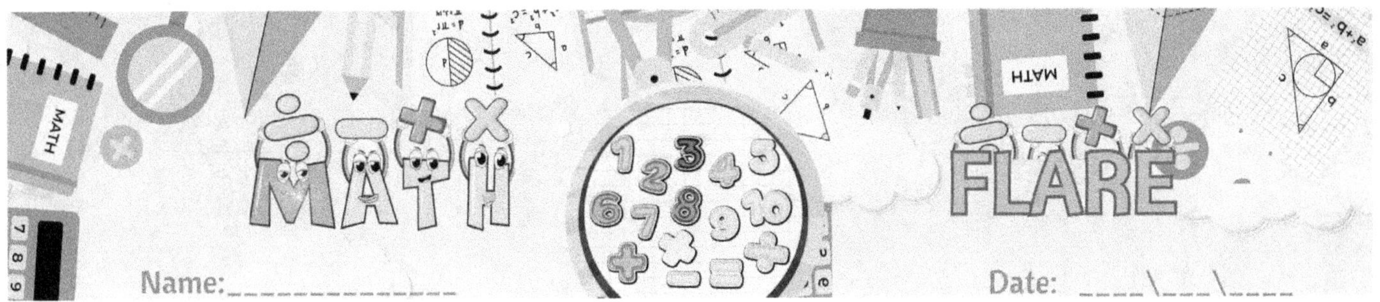

469.

✗	3	4	5	10	8	7	2	1	9	6
9									81	
10										
3						21				
8				80			16	8		
1				10	8				9	6
7						49				
6								6		
4		16	20	40						
2		8			16		4	2		
5								5		30

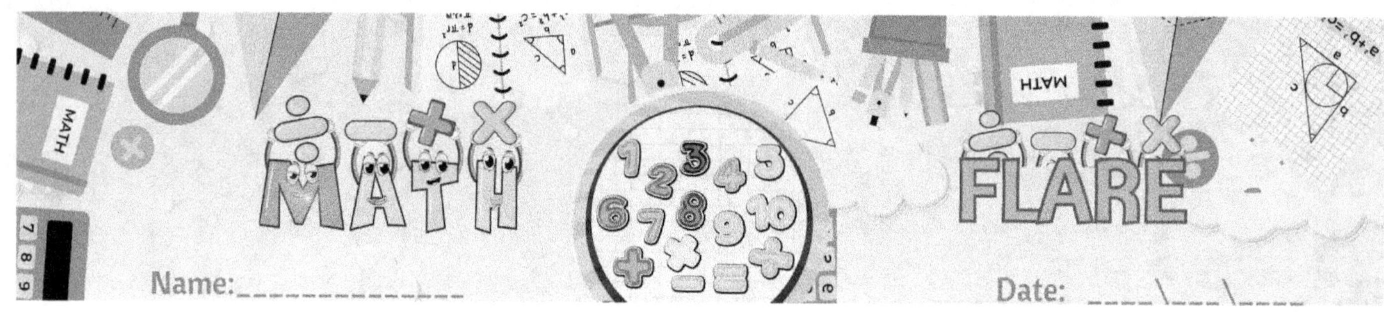

470.

×	1	2	3	9	7	4	6	5	10	8
7							42			56
2		4								16
3		6				12		15		
10							60			
1								5		
8			24						80	
4	4	8								
9	9						54		90	
6		12			42					48
5								25		

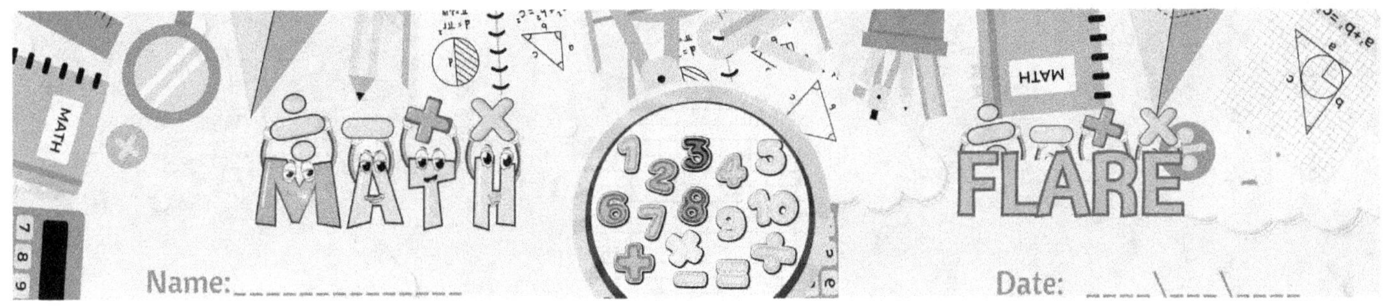

471.

×	2	1	5	6	8	7	4	10	9	3
6			30					60		
5					40				45	15
7		7	35							
10								100	90	
1		1							9	
9								90	81	
4			20	24			16			
2										
8		8								
3		3	15		24					

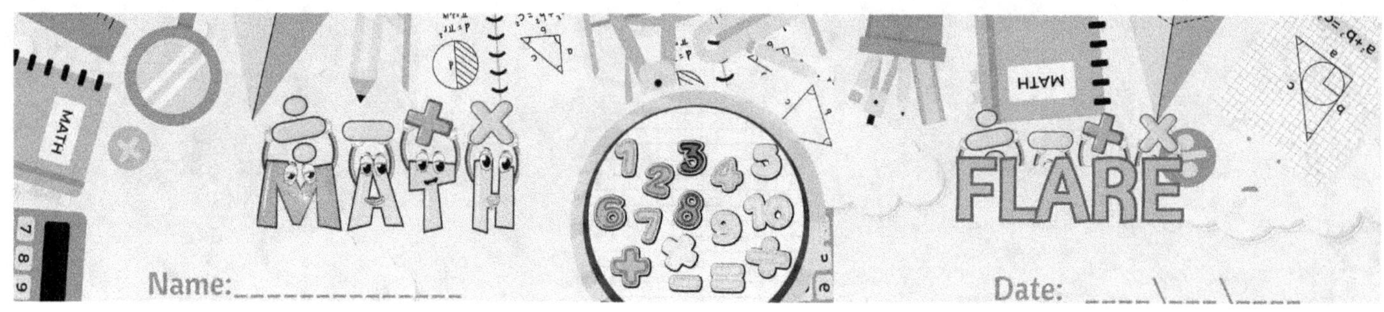

472.

×	7	8	2	10	1	5	4	9	6	3
5	35							45	30	
9						45		81		
10				100						
6		48			6					18
3			6					27		
1										
4		32						36		
8			16							
7	49		14				28			
2	14					10				6

473.

✖	2	1	10	5	6	4	3	7	8	9
1			10	5				7		
2					12					
5							15			
10			100						80	
9	18									
8	16							56	64	
7	14	7						49		
3					18					
6						24				
4	8				24	16				36

474.

×	3	4	7	8	5	1	10	9	6	2
7								63		14
3					15					
1			7					9		
2	6			10						
4								36		8
5							50			
10		40						90		
8	24		64	40						
9			63					81		
6			42	48					36	

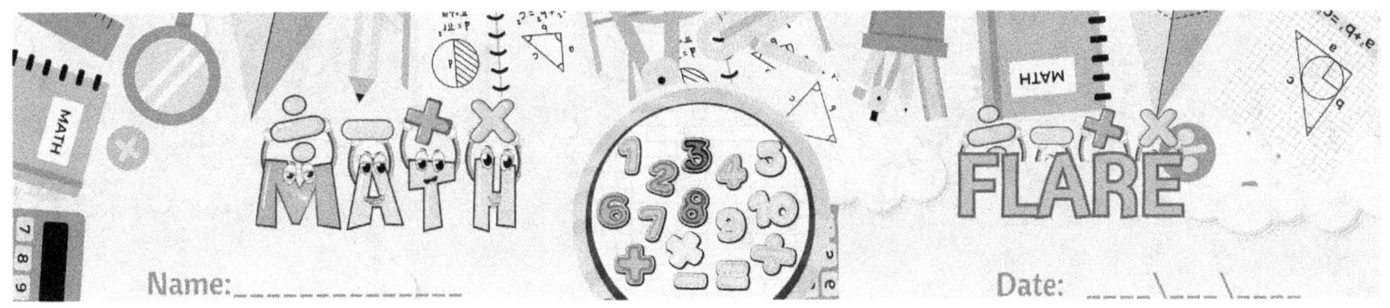

475.

×	9	3	1	6	4	10	5	8	7	2
7								56		
8										
2	18		2			10				4
4		12	4		16	40				
6								48		
9	81					90				18
3		9								6
10		30				100				
1				6						
5			5			50				

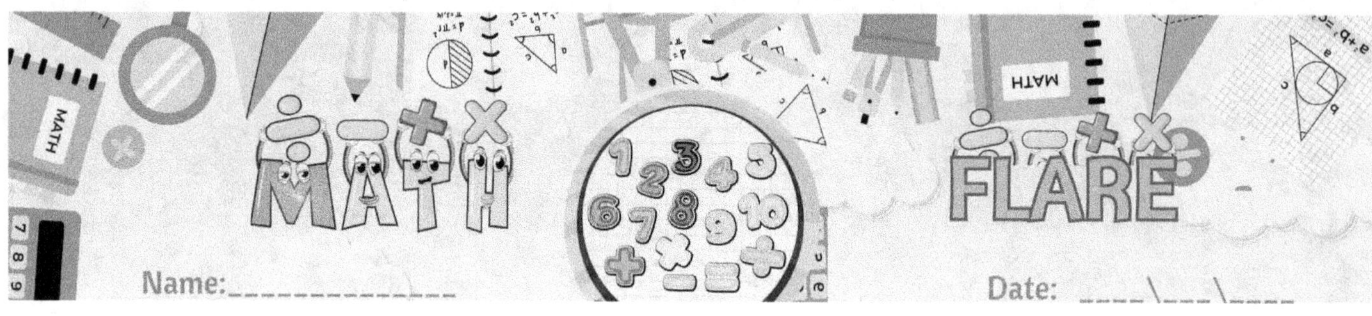

Fact Families

Complete each family of facts.

476.

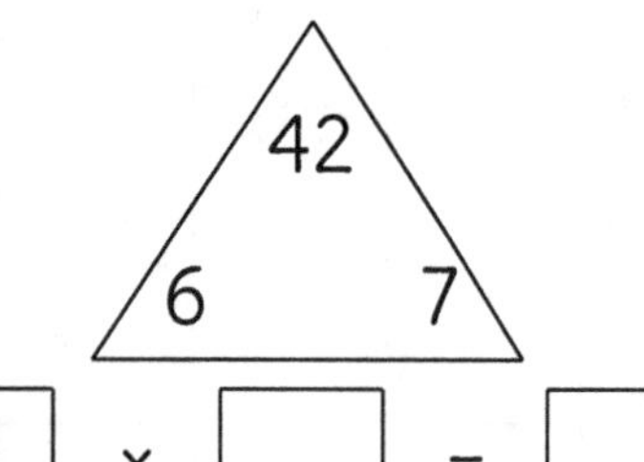

$$\square \times \square = \square$$
$$\square \times \square = \square$$
$$\square \div \square = \square$$
$$\square \div \square = \square$$

477.

$$\square \times \square = \square$$
$$\square \times \square = \square$$
$$\square \div \square = \square$$
$$\square \div \square = \square$$

478.

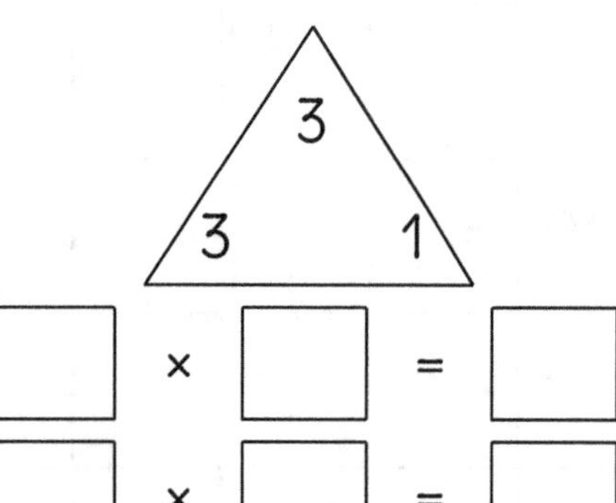

$$\square \times \square = \square$$
$$\square \times \square = \square$$
$$\square \div \square = \square$$
$$\square \div \square = \square$$

479.

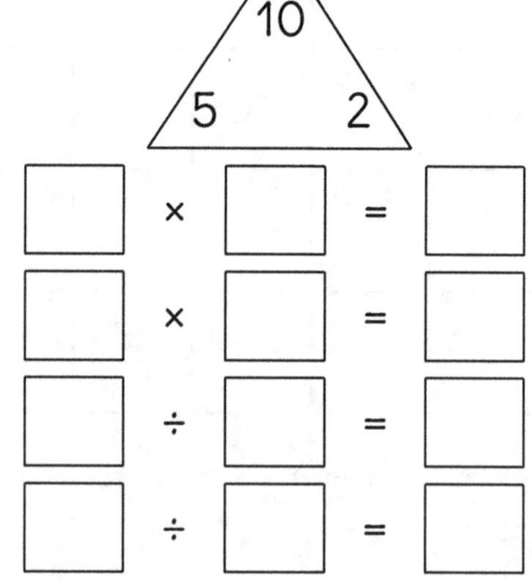

$$\square \times \square = \square$$
$$\square \times \square = \square$$
$$\square \div \square = \square$$
$$\square \div \square = \square$$

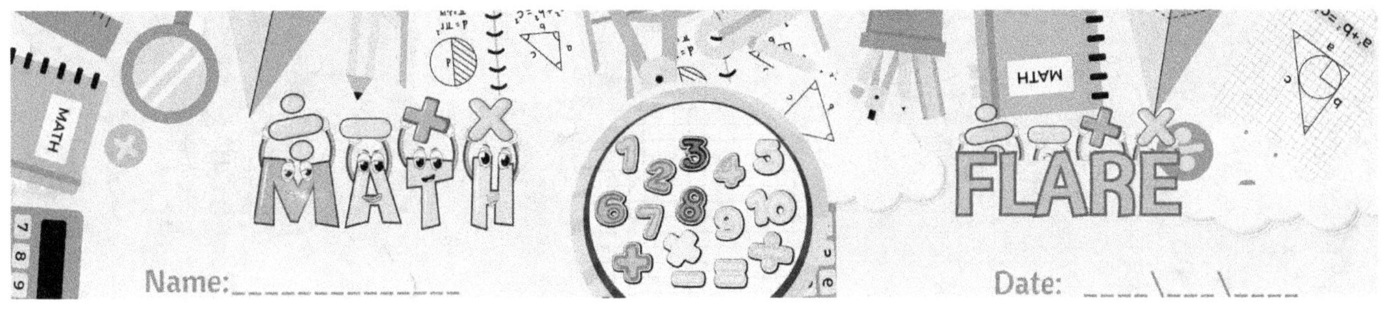

480.

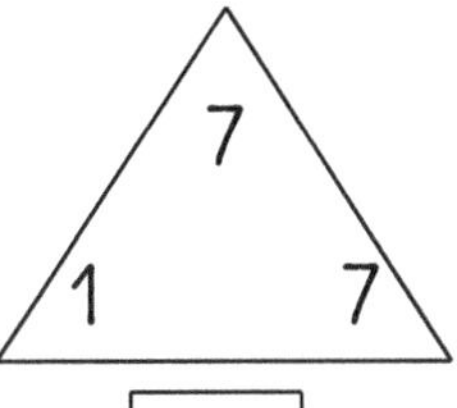

$\square \times \square = \square$

$\square \times \square = \square$

$\square \div \square = \square$

$\square \div \square = \square$

481.

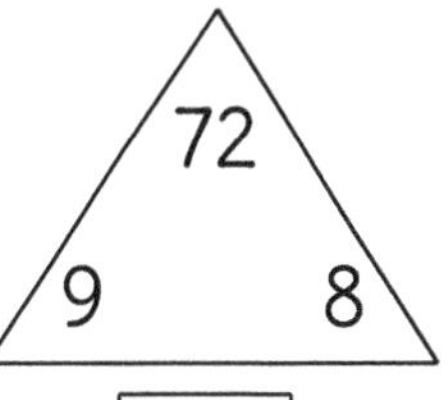

$\square \times \square = \square$

$\square \times \square = \square$

$\square \div \square = \square$

$\square \div \square = \square$

482.

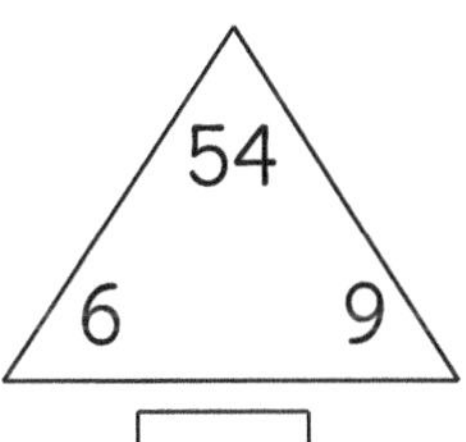

$\square \times \square = \square$

$\square \times \square = \square$

$\square \div \square = \square$

$\square \div \square = \square$

483.

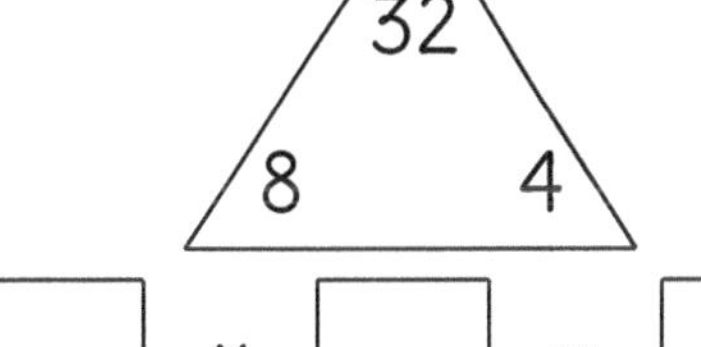

$\square \times \square = \square$

$\square \times \square = \square$

$\square \div \square = \square$

$\square \div \square = \square$

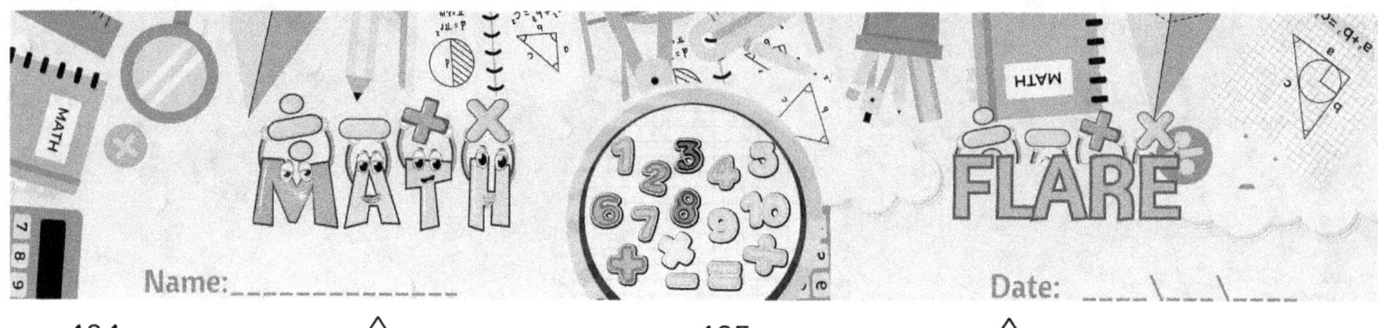

484.

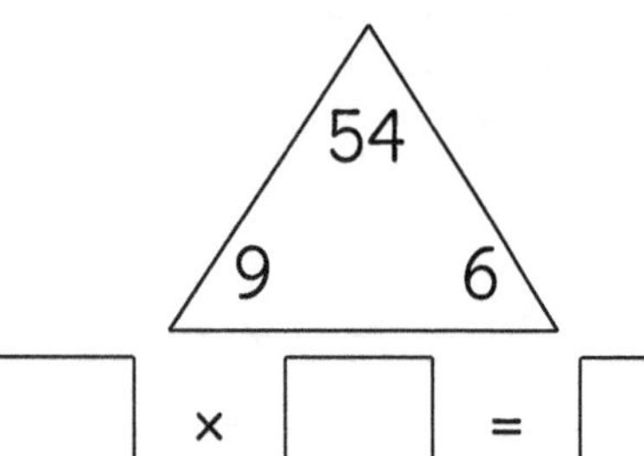

☐ × ☐ = ☐
☐ × ☐ = ☐
☐ ÷ ☐ = ☐
☐ ÷ ☐ = ☐

485.

☐ × ☐ = ☐
☐ × ☐ = ☐
☐ ÷ ☐ = ☐
☐ ÷ ☐ = ☐

486.

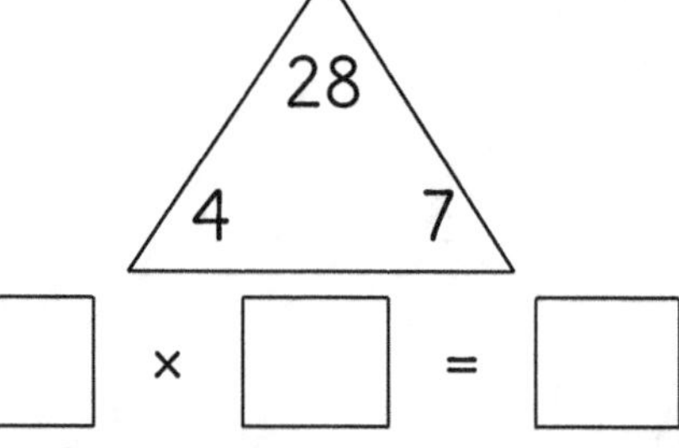

☐ × ☐ = ☐
☐ × ☐ = ☐
☐ ÷ ☐ = ☐
☐ ÷ ☐ = ☐

487.

☐ × ☐ = ☐
☐ × ☐ = ☐
☐ ÷ ☐ = ☐
☐ ÷ ☐ = ☐

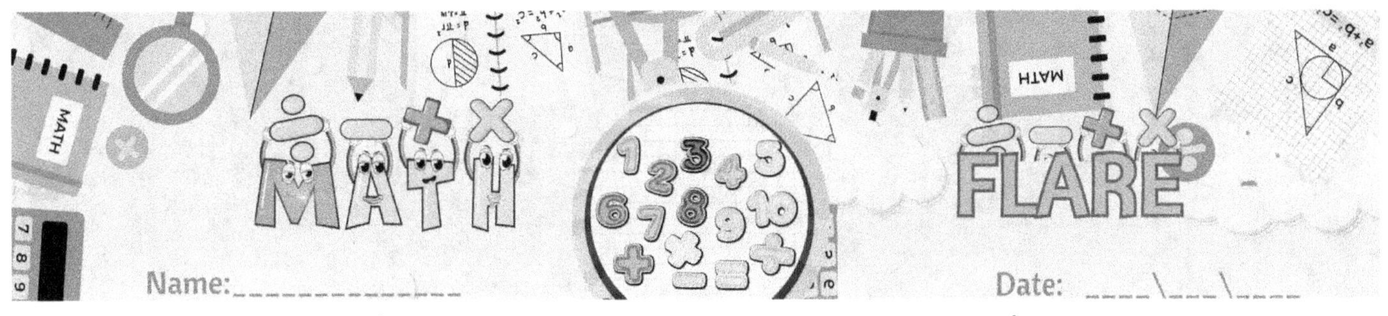

488.

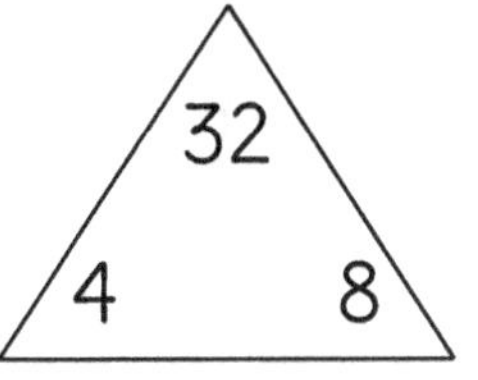

$$\square \times \square = \square$$
$$\square \times \square = \square$$
$$\square \div \square = \square$$
$$\square \div \square = \square$$

489.

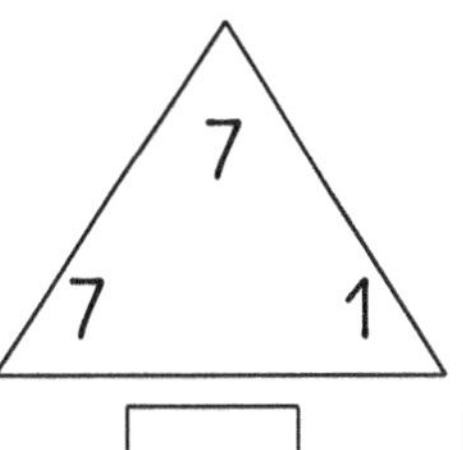

$$\square \times \square = \square$$
$$\square \times \square = \square$$
$$\square \div \square = \square$$
$$\square \div \square = \square$$

490.

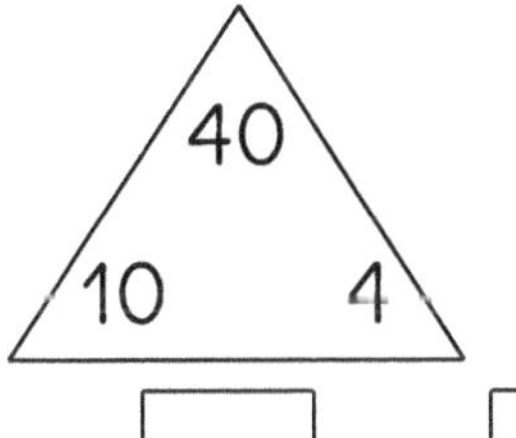

$$\square \times \square = \square$$
$$\square \times \square = \square$$
$$\square \div \square = \square$$
$$\square \div \square = \square$$

491.

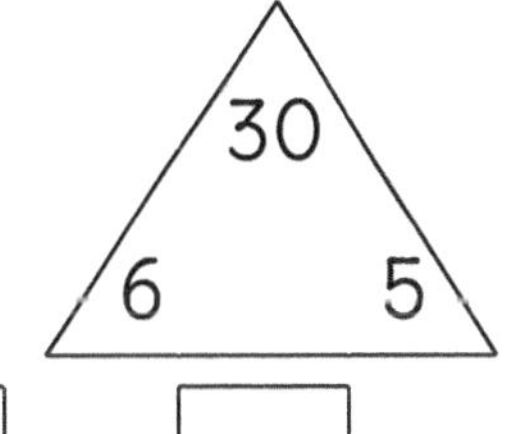

$$\square \times \square = \square$$
$$\square \times \square = \square$$
$$\square \div \square = \square$$
$$\square \div \square = \square$$

492.

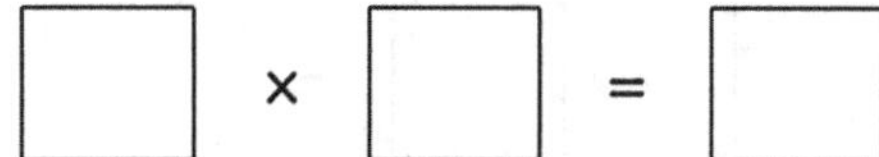

28
7   4

☐ × ☐ = ☐
☐ × ☐ = ☐
☐ ÷ ☐ = ☐
☐ ÷ ☐ = ☐

493.

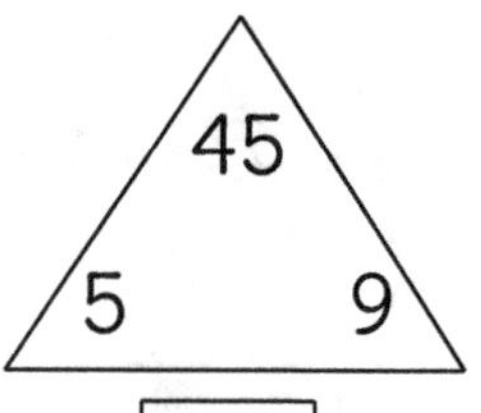

45
5   9

☐ × ☐ = ☐
☐ × ☐ = ☐
☐ ÷ ☐ = ☐
☐ ÷ ☐ = ☐

494.

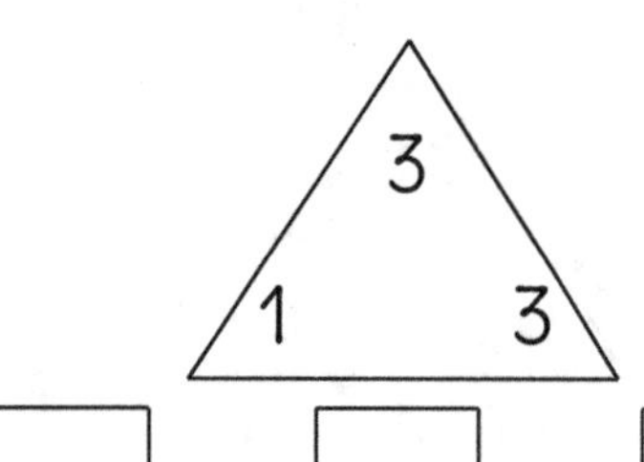

3
1   3

☐ × ☐ = ☐
☐ × ☐ = ☐
☐ ÷ ☐ = ☐
☐ ÷ ☐ = ☐

495.

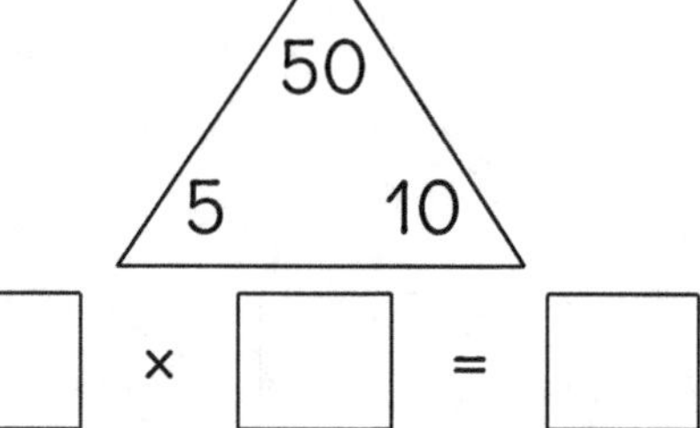

50
5   10

☐ × ☐ = ☐
☐ × ☐ = ☐
☐ ÷ ☐ = ☐
☐ ÷ ☐ = ☐

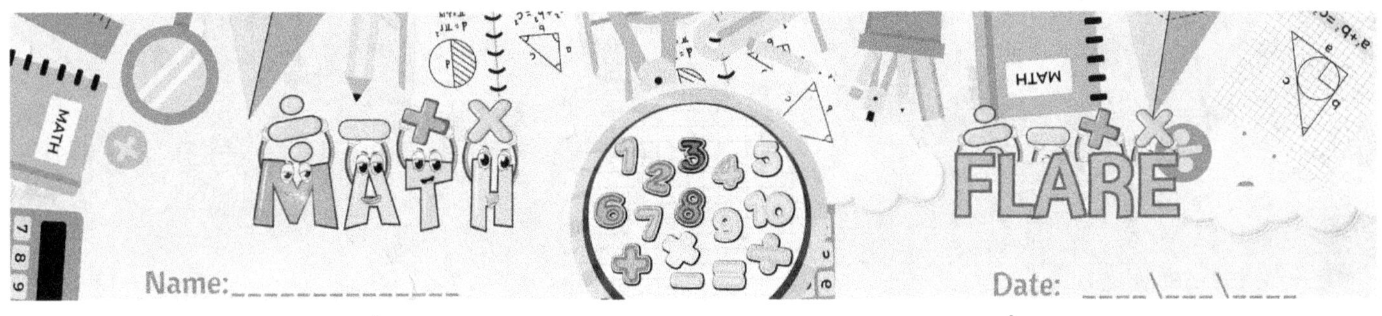

496.

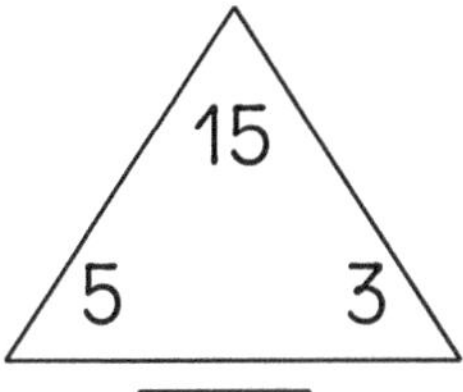

[ ] × [ ] = [ ]

[ ] × [ ] = [ ]

[ ] ÷ [ ] = [ ]

[ ] ÷ [ ] = [ ]

497.

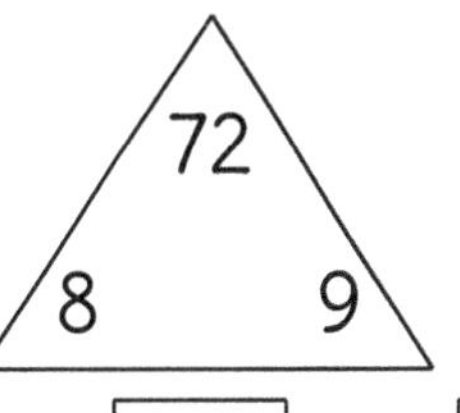

[ ] × [ ] = [ ]

[ ] × [ ] = [ ]

[ ] ÷ [ ] = [ ]

[ ] ÷ [ ] = [ ]

498.

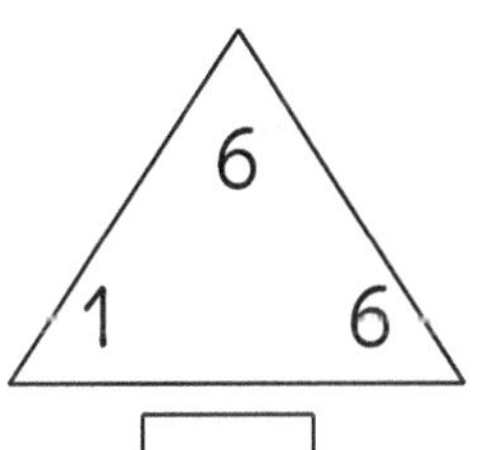

[ ] × [ ] = [ ]

[ ] × [ ] = [ ]

[ ] ÷ [ ] = [ ]

[ ] ÷ [ ] = [ ]

499.

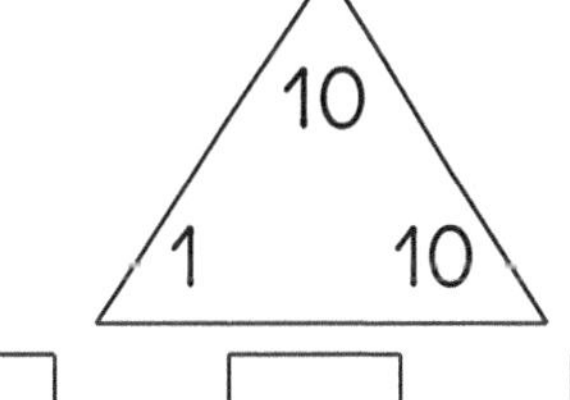

[ ] × [ ] = [ ]

[ ] × [ ] = [ ]

[ ] ÷ [ ] = [ ]

[ ] ÷ [ ] = [ ]

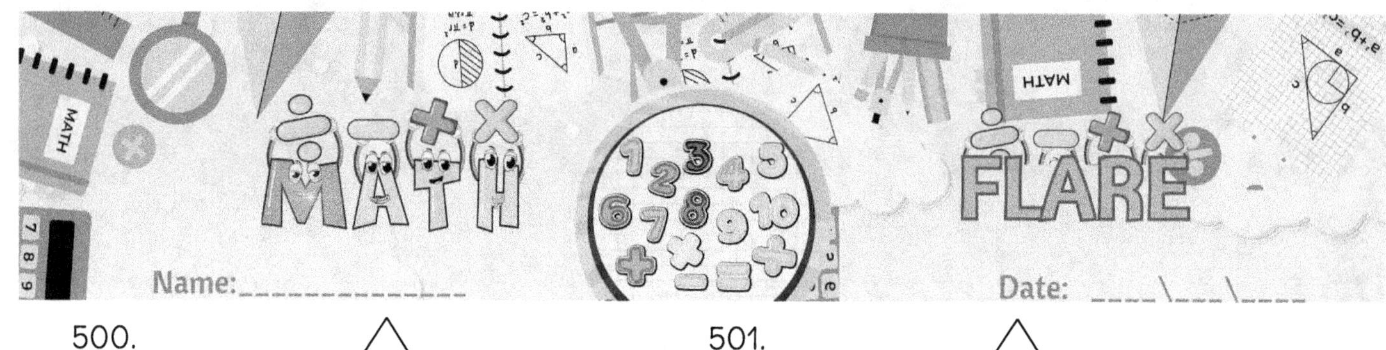

500.

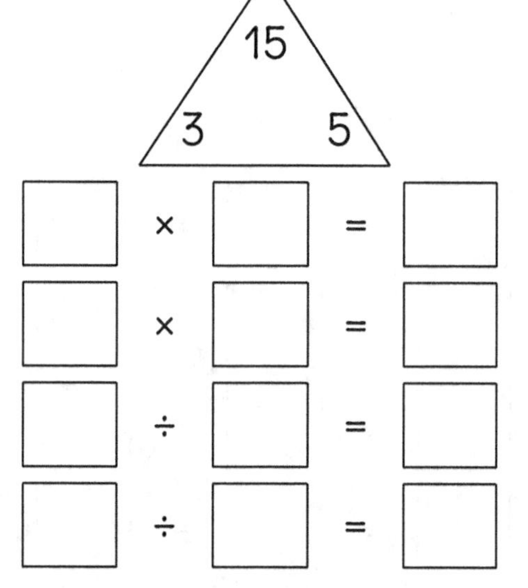

14
7   2

[ ] × [ ] = [ ]
[ ] × [ ] = [ ]
[ ] ÷ [ ] = [ ]
[ ] ÷ [ ] = [ ]

501.

15
3   5

[ ] × [ ] = [ ]
[ ] × [ ] = [ ]
[ ] ÷ [ ] = [ ]
[ ] ÷ [ ] = [ ]

502.

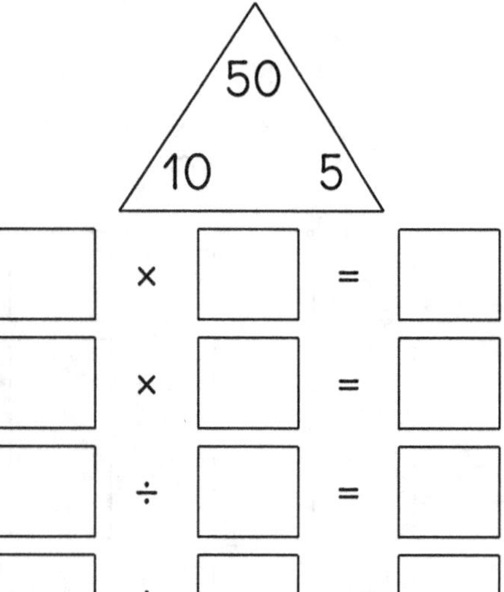

50
10   5

[ ] × [ ] = [ ]
[ ] × [ ] = [ ]
[ ] ÷ [ ] = [ ]
[ ] ÷ [ ] = [ ]

503.

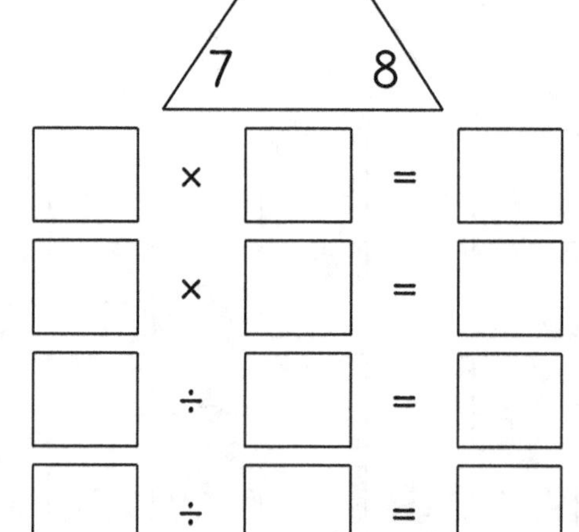

56
7   8

[ ] × [ ] = [ ]
[ ] × [ ] = [ ]
[ ] ÷ [ ] = [ ]
[ ] ÷ [ ] = [ ]

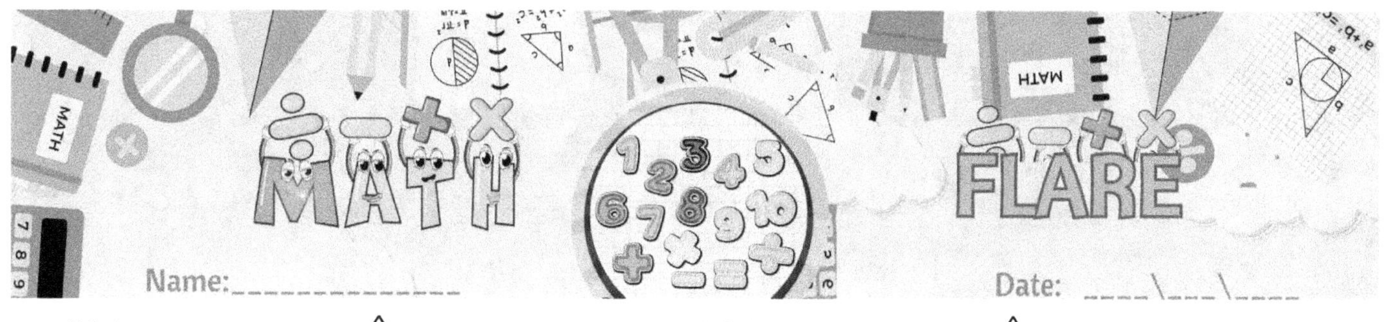

504.

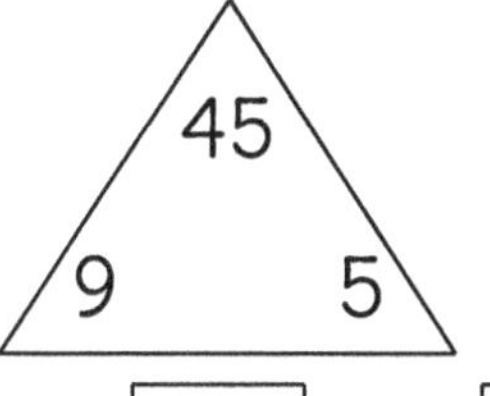

☐ × ☐ = ☐

☐ × ☐ = ☐

☐ ÷ ☐ = ☐

☐ ÷ ☐ = ☐

505.

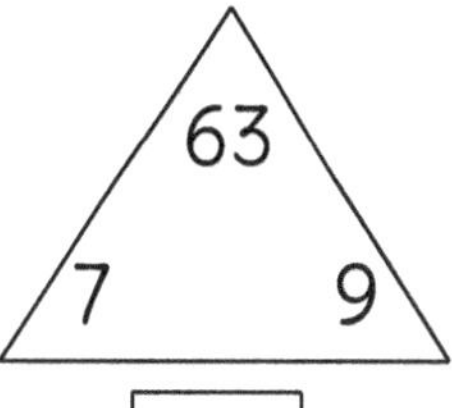

☐ × ☐ = ☐

☐ × ☐ = ☐

☐ ÷ ☐ = ☐

☐ ÷ ☐ = ☐

506.

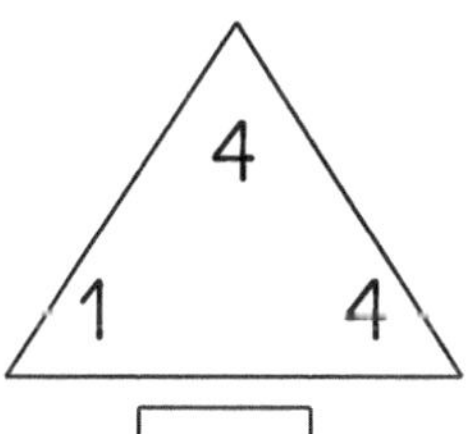

☐ × ☐ = ☐

☐ × ☐ = ☐

☐ ÷ ☐ = ☐

☐ ÷ ☐ = ☐

507.

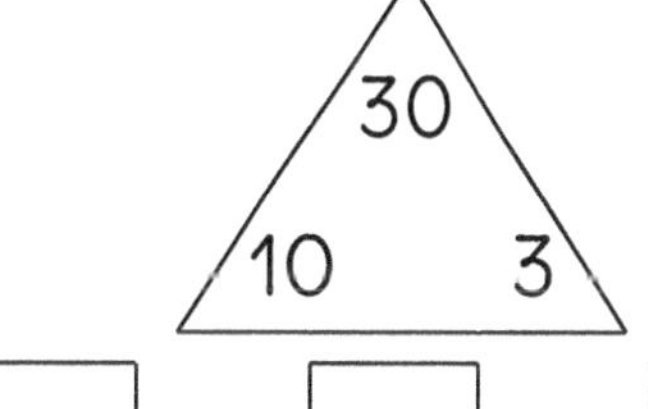

☐ × ☐ = ☐

☐ × ☐ = ☐

☐ ÷ ☐ = ☐

☐ ÷ ☐ = ☐

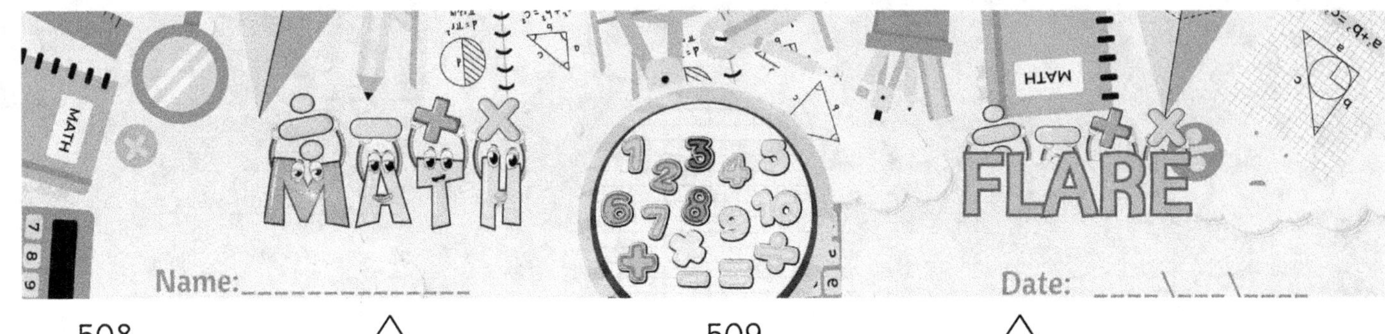

508.

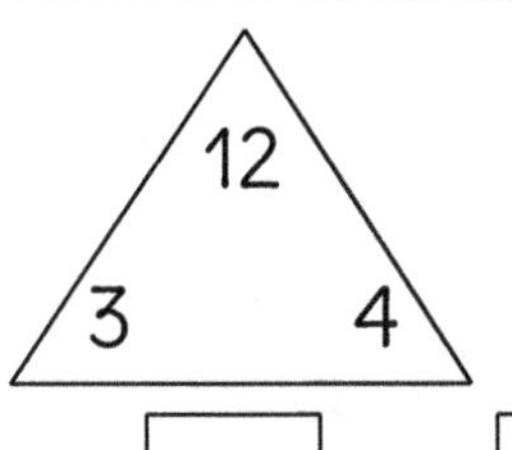

☐	×	☐	=	☐
☐	×	☐	=	☐
☐	÷	☐	=	☐
☐	÷	☐	=	☐

509.

☐	×	☐	=	☐
☐	×	☐	=	☐
☐	÷	☐	=	☐
☐	÷	☐	=	☐

510.

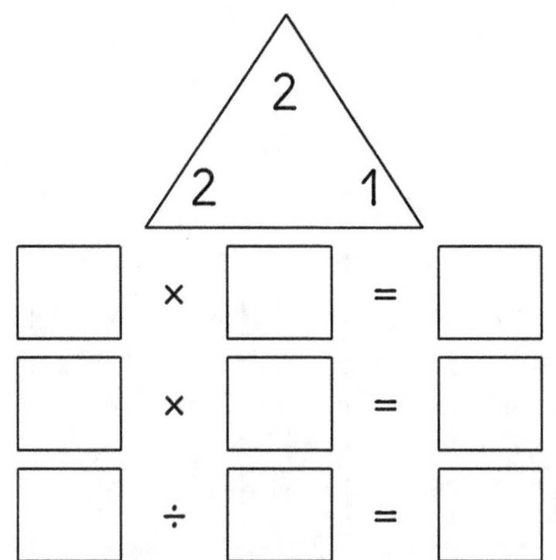

☐	×	☐	=	☐
☐	×	☐	=	☐
☐	÷	☐	=	☐
☐	÷	☐	=	☐

511.

☐	×	☐	=	☐
☐	×	☐	=	☐
☐	÷	☐	=	☐
☐	÷	☐	=	☐

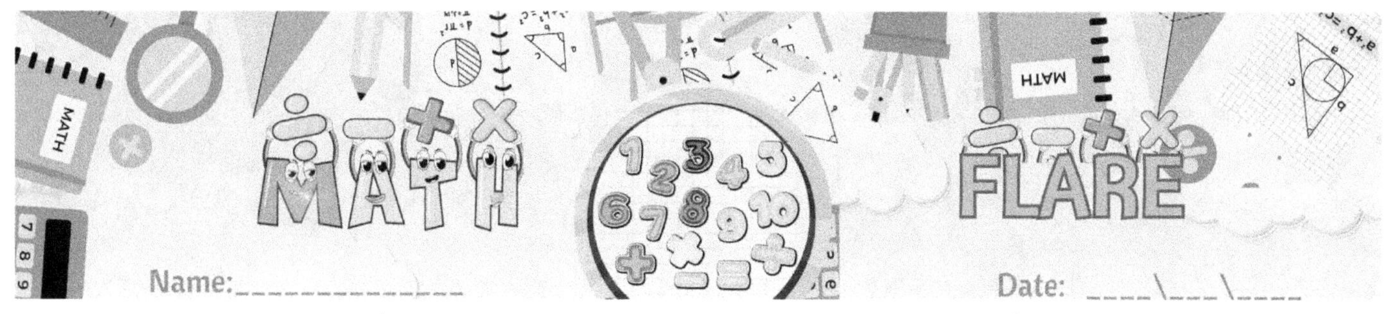

512.

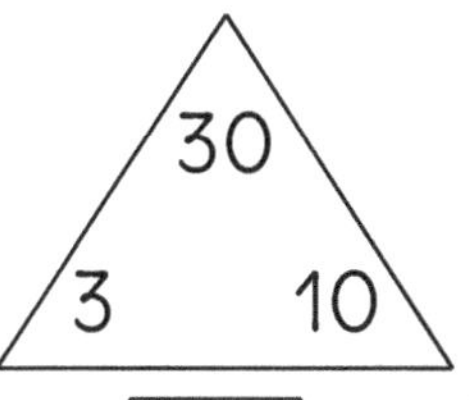

☐ × ☐ = ☐

☐ × ☐ = ☐

☐ ÷ ☐ = ☐

☐ ÷ ☐ = ☐

513.

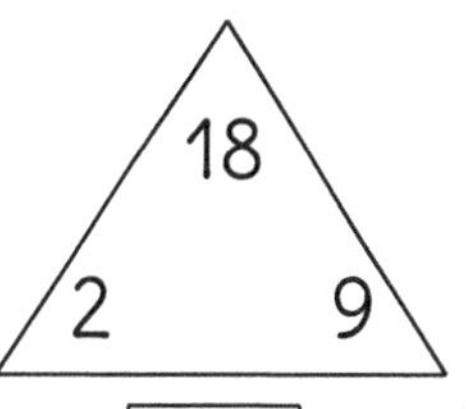

☐ × ☐ = ☐

☐ × ☐ = ☐

☐ ÷ ☐ = ☐

☐ ÷ ☐ = ☐

514.

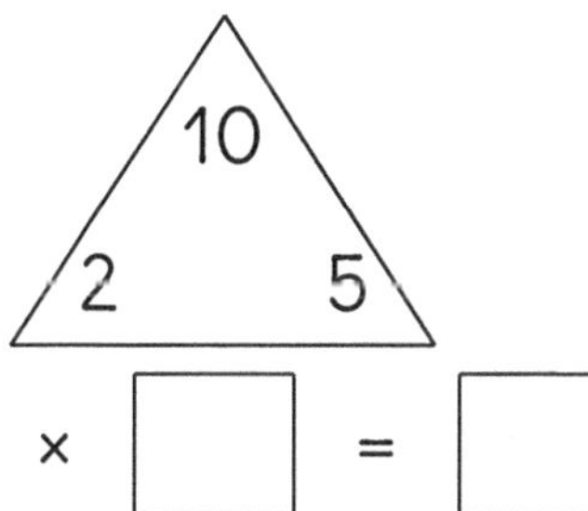

☐ × ☐ = ☐

☐ × ☐ = ☐

☐ ÷ ☐ = ☐

☐ ÷ ☐ = ☐

515.

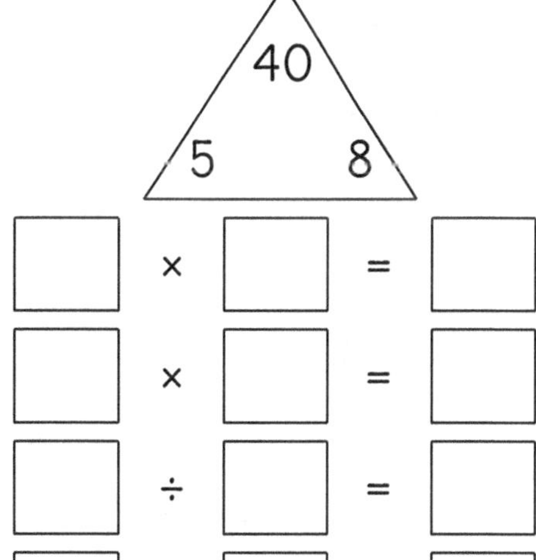

☐ × ☐ = ☐

☐ × ☐ = ☐

☐ ÷ ☐ = ☐

☐ ÷ ☐ = ☐

ANSWERS

Page 1:   Multiplication by 1

1. 5   2. 2   3. 6   4. 4   5. 3   6. 7   7. 8   8. 9   9. 1   10. 2   11. 6

12. 3   13. 7   14. 5   15. 8   16. 4   17. 9   18. 6   19. 4   20. 1

Page 2:   Multiplication by 2

21. 8   22. 16   23. 12   24. 6   25. 2   26. 4   27. 10   28. 18   29. 14

30. 2   31. 8   32. 10   33. 6   34. 18   35. 14   36. 12   37. 16   38. 12

39. 14   40. 16

Page 3:   Multiplication by 3

41. 3   42. 18   43. 9   44. 21   45. 12   46. 6   47. 24   48. 15

49. 27   50. 24   51. 21   52. 3   53. 27   54. 15   55. 12   56. 6

57. 18   58. 24   59. 27   60. 24

Page 4:   Multiplication by 4

61. 12   62. 16   63. 20   64. 28   65. 24   66. 4   67. 32   68. 36

69. 8   70. 24   71. 20   72. 28   73. 12   74. 32   75. 36   76. 8

77. 4   78. 36   79. 16   80. 8

Page 5:   Multiplication by 5

81. 25   82. 10   83. 15   84. 20   85. 40   86. 45   87. 35

88. 5   89. 30   90. 40   91. 15   92. 45   93. 20   94. 10

95. 30   96. 35   97. 5   98. 35   99. 20   100. 35

Page 6:   Multiplication by 6

101. 48   102. 18   103. 30   104. 42   105. 12   106. 36   107. 6

108. 24   109. 54   110. 18   111. 54   112. 30   113. 42   114. 12

115. 48   116. 24   117. 6   118. 12   119. 6   120. 30

Page 7: Multiplication by 7

121. 56   122. 42   123. 28   124. 7   125. 21   126. 35   127. 49   128. 14

129. 63   130. 21   131. 28   132. 63   133. 56   134. 42   135. 35   136. 14

137. 7   138. 28   139. 49   140. 14

Page 8: Multiplication by 8

141. 56   142. 40   143. 24   144. 64   145. 16   146. 32   147. 8   148. 48

149. 72   150. 56   151. 40   152. 16   153. 72   154. 24   155. 32   156. 8

157. 48   158. 40   159. 72   160. 56

Page 9: Multiplication by 9

161. 54   162. 36   163. 9   164. 63   165. 72   166. 45   167. 18   168. 27

169. 81   170. 63   171. 27   172. 72   173. 54   174. 9   175. 36   176. 18

177. 45   178. 27   179. 72   180. 18

Page 10: Multiplication by 10

181. 30   182. 40   183. 60   184. 80   185. 50   186. 10   187. 70

188. 20   189. 90   190. 20   191. 50   192. 30   193. 80   194. 60

195. 10   196. 70   197. 90   198. 40   199. 40   200. 40

Page 11: Basic Multiplication

201. 16   202. 48   203. 4   204. 5   205. 6   206. 20

207. 50   208. 28   209. 8   210. 48   211. 27   212. 45

213. 36   214. 21   215. 24   216. 12   217. 63   218. 80

219. 10   220. 6   221. 90   222. 32   223. 80   224. 16

225. 63   226. 15   227. 5   228. 16   229. 40   230. 32

231. 12   232. 18   233. 30   234. 56   235. 50   236. 14

237. 4   238. 25   239. 18   240. 72   241. 7   242. 18

243. 56   244. 12   245. 72   246. 10   247. 3   248. 30

249. 1   250. 45   251. 8   252. 40   253. 6   254. 20

255. 35   256. 35   257. 42   258. 9   259. 10   260. 42

261. 14   262. 15   263. 4   264. 54   265. 36   266. 9

267. 7   268. 40   269. 30   270. 8   271. 12   272. 54

273. 30   274. 49   275. 18   276. 28   277. 10   278. 24

279. 90   280. 8   281. 81   282. 2   283. 64   284. 24

285. 36   286. 9   287. 27   288. 100   289. 20   290. 60

291. 2   292. 70   293. 24   294. 60   295. 3   296. 6

297. 20   298. 21   299. 70   300. 40

Page 16: Basic Multiplication

301. 80   302. 49   303. 54   304. 40   305. 24   306. 18   307. 5

308. 12   309. 48   310. 15   311. 16   312. 6   313. 9   314. 24

315. 45   316. 24   317. 60   318. 18   319. 54   320. 27   321. 14

322. 35   323. 16   324. 2   325. 32   326. 18   327. 20   328. 8

329. 6   330. 40   331. 27   332. 48   333. 60   334. 42   335. 35

336. 64   337. 10   338. 4   339. 36   340. 16   341. 63   342. 36

343. 3   344. 56   345. 30   346. 42   347. 6   348. 25   349. 56

350. 7   351. 20   352. 45   353. 15   354. 10   355. 10   356. 24

357. 12   358. 10   359. 28   360. 12   361. 81   362. 40   363. 18

364. 32   365. 90   366. 5   367. 8   368. 90   369. 4   370. 50

371. 8   372. 8   373. 21   374. 21   375. 4   376. 9   377. 2

378. 63   379. 30   380. 70   381. 28   382. 72   383. 6   384. 40

385. 70   386. 80   387. 20   388. 30   389. 12   390. 50   391. 30

392. 36   393. 14

Page 19: Commutative Property

394. 8   395. 7   396. 6   397. 5   398. 5   399. 3   400. 5   401. 6

402. 8   403. 5   404. 3   405. 5   406. 2   407. 7   408. 6   409. 7

410. 3   411. 10   412. 2   413. 1   414. 2   415. 2   416. 1   417. 6

418. 9   419. 2   420. 9   421. 2   422. 2   423. 5   424. 6   425. 9

426. 7   427. 3   428. 1   429. 9   430. 1   431. 3   432. 10   433. 8

434. 1   435. 8   436. 3   437. 6   438. 3   439. 4   440. 6   441. 1

442. 5   443. 5   444. 7   445. 2

Page 22: Matching the answers.

446. a.F b.B c.I d.C e.E f.G g.D h.J i.A j.H

447. a.C b.A c.I d.D e.B f.E g.G h.J i.F j.H

448. a.G b.H c.F d.C e.A f.J g.B h.E i.I j.D

449. a.A b.F c.I d.C e.D f.J g.B h.E i.H j.G

450. a.A b.J c.I d.D e.G f.C g.H h.E i.F j.B

451. a.H b.I c.F d.D e.B f.A g.J h.G i.C j.E

452. a.A b.F c.E d.H e.D f.J g.C h.I i.G j.B

453. a.E b.B c.F d.G e.J f.A g.I h.C i.D j.H

454. a.H b.I c.A d.B e.F f.D g.E h.J i.C j.G

455. a.J b.B c.F d.A e.E f.C g.I h.G i.H j.D

Page 32:   Multiplication Circles

456.   457.   458.

459.   460.   461.

462.   463.   464.

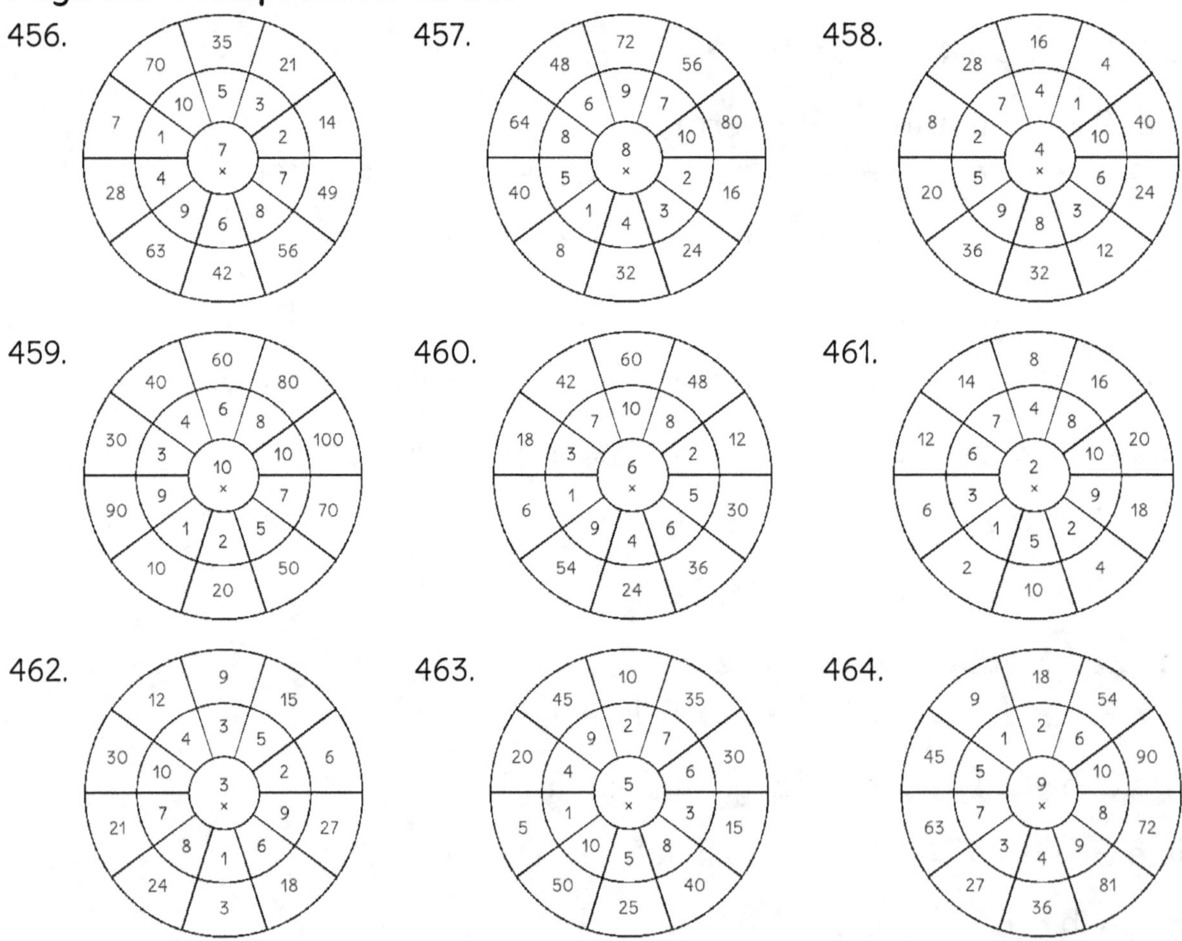

465.

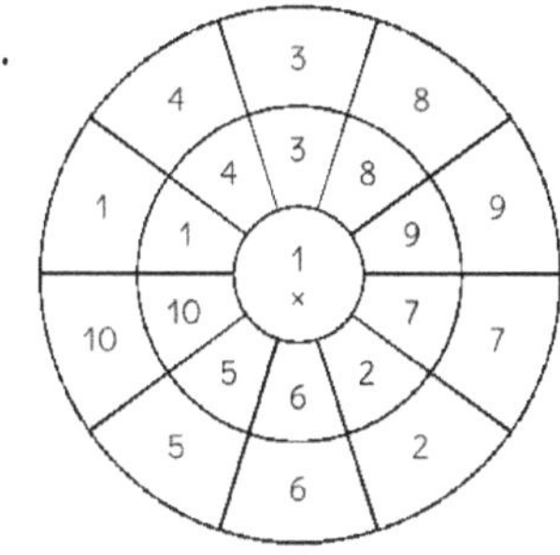

Page 37:   Table-Drill Multiplication

466.

×	3	5	9	4	8	10	6	7	1	2
8	24	40	72	32	64	80	48	56	8	16
7	21	35	63	28	56	70	42	49	7	14
5	15	25	45	20	40	50	30	35	5	10
1	3	5	9	4	8	10	6	7	1	2
4	12	20	36	16	32	40	24	28	4	8
6	18	30	54	24	48	60	36	42	6	12
3	9	15	27	12	24	30	18	21	3	6
9	27	45	81	36	72	90	54	63	9	18
2	6	10	18	8	16	20	12	14	2	4
10	30	50	90	40	80	100	60	70	10	20

467.

×	1	2	6	5	9	4	7	8	3	10
1	1	2	6	5	9	4	7	8	3	10
6	6	12	36	30	54	24	42	48	18	60
4	4	8	24	20	36	16	28	32	12	40
8	8	16	48	40	72	32	56	64	24	80
10	10	20	60	50	90	40	70	80	30	100
7	7	14	42	35	63	28	49	56	21	70
2	2	4	12	10	18	8	14	16	6	20
5	5	10	30	25	45	20	35	40	15	50
9	9	18	54	45	81	36	63	72	27	90
3	3	6	18	15	27	12	21	24	9	30

468.

×	6	4	8	1	7	2	5	3	9	10
5	30	20	40	5	35	10	25	15	45	50
3	18	12	24	3	21	6	15	9	27	30
6	36	24	48	6	42	12	30	18	54	60
7	42	28	56	7	49	14	35	21	63	70
9	54	36	72	9	63	18	45	27	81	90
2	12	8	16	2	14	4	10	6	18	20
10	60	40	80	10	70	20	50	30	90	100
1	6	4	8	1	7	2	5	3	9	10
8	48	32	64	8	56	16	40	24	72	80
4	24	16	32	4	28	8	20	12	36	40

469.

×	3	4	5	10	8	7	2	1	9	6
9	27	36	45	90	72	63	18	9	81	54
10	30	40	50	100	80	70	20	10	90	60
3	9	12	15	30	24	21	6	3	27	18
8	24	32	40	80	64	56	16	8	72	48
1	3	4	5	10	8	7	2	1	9	6
7	21	28	35	70	56	49	14	7	63	42
6	18	24	30	60	48	42	12	6	54	36
4	12	16	20	40	32	28	8	4	36	24
2	6	8	10	20	16	14	4	2	18	12
5	15	20	25	50	40	35	10	5	45	30

470.

×	1	2	3	9	7	4	6	5	10	8
7	7	14	21	63	49	28	42	35	70	56
2	2	4	6	18	14	8	12	10	20	16
3	3	6	9	27	21	12	18	15	30	24
10	10	20	30	90	70	40	60	50	100	80
1	1	2	3	9	7	4	6	5	10	8
8	8	16	24	72	56	32	48	40	80	64
4	4	8	12	36	28	16	24	20	40	32
9	9	18	27	81	63	36	54	45	90	72
6	6	12	18	54	42	24	36	30	60	48
5	5	10	15	45	35	20	30	25	50	40

471.

×	2	1	5	6	8	7	4	10	9	3
6	12	6	30	36	48	42	24	60	54	18
5	10	5	25	30	40	35	20	50	45	15
7	14	7	35	42	56	49	28	70	63	21
10	20	10	50	60	80	70	40	100	90	30
1	2	1	5	6	8	7	4	10	9	3
9	18	9	45	54	72	63	36	90	81	27
4	8	4	20	24	32	28	16	40	36	12
2	4	2	10	12	16	14	8	20	18	6
8	16	8	40	48	64	56	32	80	72	24
3	6	3	15	18	24	21	12	30	27	9

472.

×	7	8	2	10	1	5	4	9	6	3
5	35	40	10	50	5	25	20	45	30	15
9	63	72	18	90	9	45	36	81	54	27
10	70	80	20	100	10	50	40	90	60	30
6	42	48	12	60	6	30	24	54	36	18
3	21	24	6	30	3	15	12	27	18	9
1	7	8	2	10	1	5	4	9	6	3
4	28	32	8	40	4	20	16	36	24	12
8	56	64	16	80	8	40	32	72	48	24
7	49	56	14	70	7	35	28	63	42	21
2	14	16	4	20	2	10	8	18	12	6

473.

×	2	1	10	5	6	4	3	7	8	9
1	2	1	10	5	6	4	3	7	8	9
2	4	2	20	10	12	8	6	14	16	18
5	10	5	50	25	30	20	15	35	40	45
10	20	10	100	50	60	40	30	70	80	90
9	18	9	90	45	54	36	27	63	72	81
8	16	8	80	40	48	32	24	56	64	72
7	14	7	70	35	42	28	21	49	56	63
3	6	3	30	15	18	12	9	21	24	27
6	12	6	60	30	36	24	18	42	48	54
4	8	4	40	20	24	16	12	28	32	36

474.

×	3	4	7	8	5	1	10	9	6	2
7	21	28	49	56	35	7	70	63	42	14
3	9	12	21	24	15	3	30	27	18	6
1	3	4	7	8	5	1	10	9	6	2
2	6	8	14	16	10	2	20	18	12	4
4	12	16	28	32	20	4	40	36	24	8
5	15	20	35	40	25	5	50	45	30	10
10	30	40	70	80	50	10	100	90	60	20
8	24	32	56	64	40	8	80	72	48	16
9	27	36	63	72	45	9	90	81	54	18
6	18	24	42	48	30	6	60	54	36	12

475.

×	9	3	1	6	4	10	5	8	7	2
7	63	21	7	42	28	70	35	56	49	14
8	72	24	8	48	32	80	40	64	56	16
2	18	6	2	12	8	20	10	16	14	4
4	36	12	4	24	16	40	20	32	28	8
6	54	18	6	36	24	60	30	48	42	12
9	81	27	9	54	36	90	45	72	63	18
3	27	9	3	18	12	30	15	24	21	6
10	90	30	10	60	40	100	50	80	70	20
1	9	3	1	6	4	10	5	8	7	2
5	45	15	5	30	20	50	25	40	35	10

Page 47:   Fact Families

476.

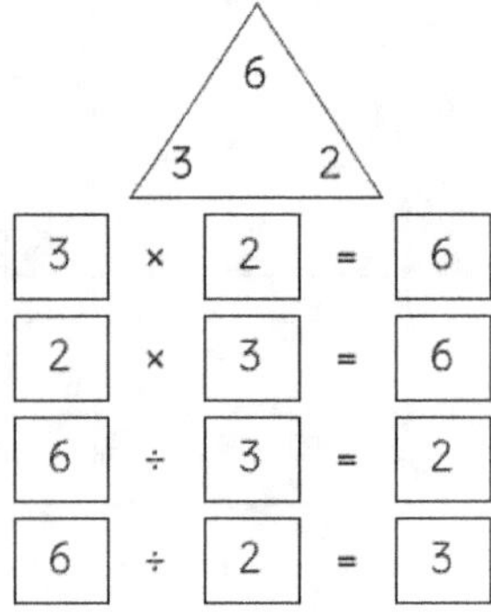

$$6 \times 7 = 42$$
$$7 \times 6 = 42$$
$$42 \div 6 = 7$$
$$42 \div 7 = 6$$

477.

$$3 \times 2 = 6$$
$$2 \times 3 = 6$$
$$6 \div 3 = 2$$
$$6 \div 2 = 3$$

478.

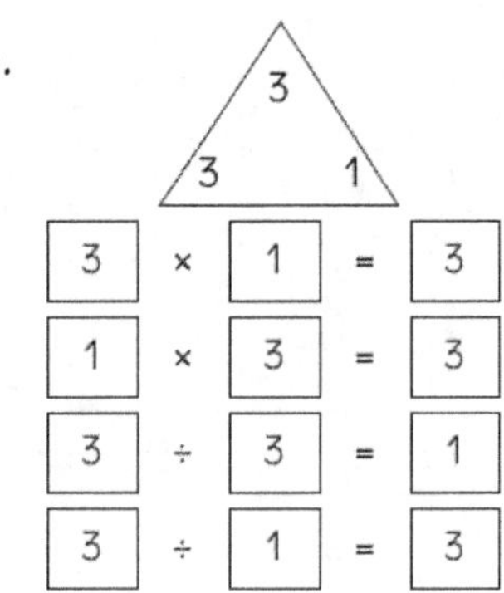

$$3 \times 1 = 3$$
$$1 \times 3 = 3$$
$$3 \div 3 = 1$$
$$3 \div 1 = 3$$

479.

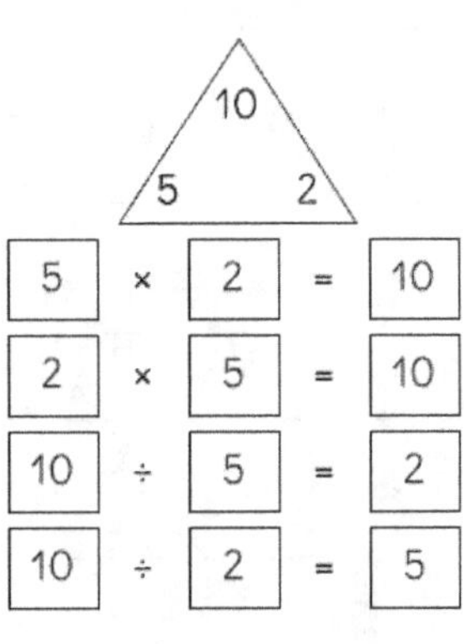

$$5 \times 2 = 10$$
$$2 \times 5 = 10$$
$$10 \div 5 = 2$$
$$10 \div 2 = 5$$

480.

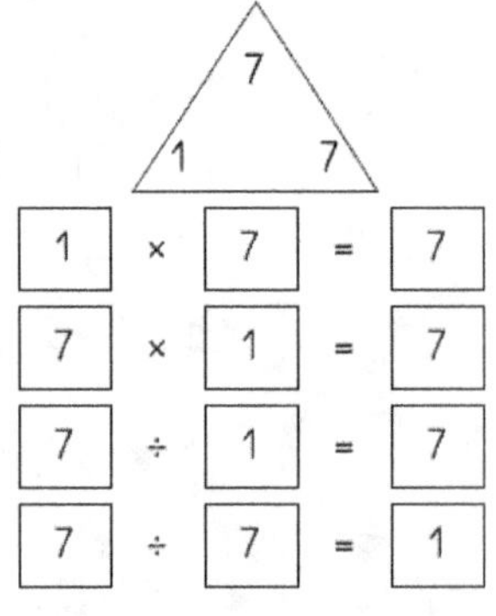

$$1 \times 7 = 7$$
$$7 \times 1 = 7$$
$$7 \div 1 = 7$$
$$7 \div 7 = 1$$

481.

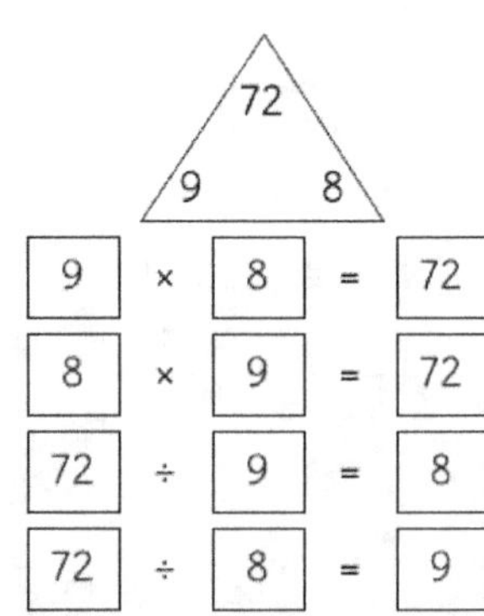

$$9 \times 8 = 72$$
$$8 \times 9 = 72$$
$$72 \div 9 = 8$$
$$72 \div 8 = 9$$

482. 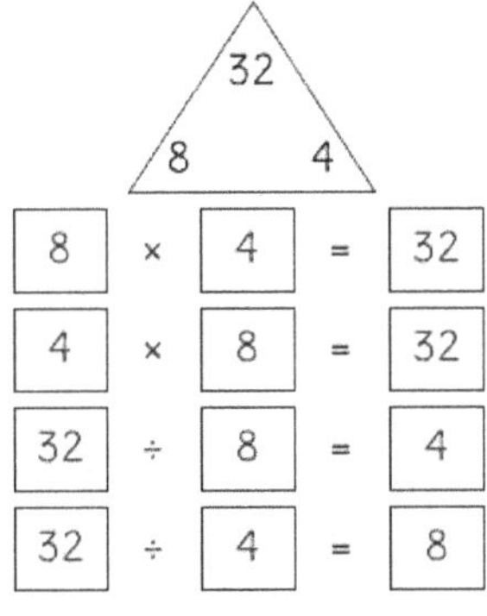

6	×	9	=	54
9	×	6	=	54
54	÷	6	=	9
54	÷	9	=	6

483. 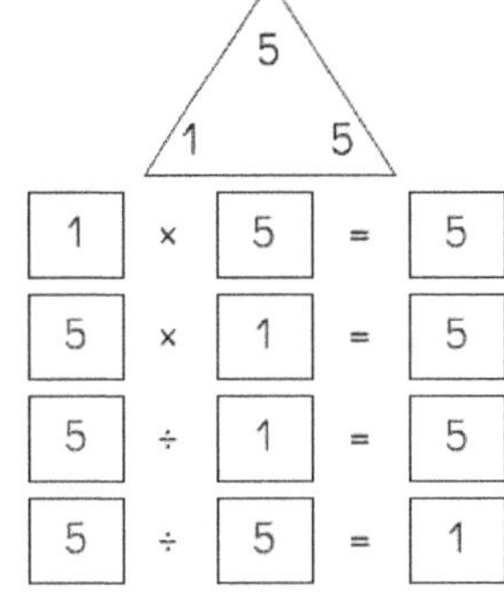

8	×	4	=	32
4	×	8	=	32
32	÷	8	=	4
32	÷	4	=	8

484.

1	×	5	=	5
5	×	1	=	5
5	÷	1	=	5
5	÷	5	=	1

485. 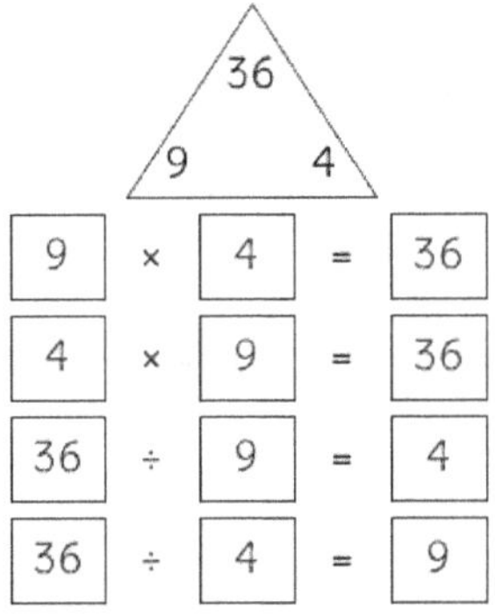

9	×	4	=	36
4	×	9	=	36
36	÷	9	=	4
36	÷	4	=	9

486. 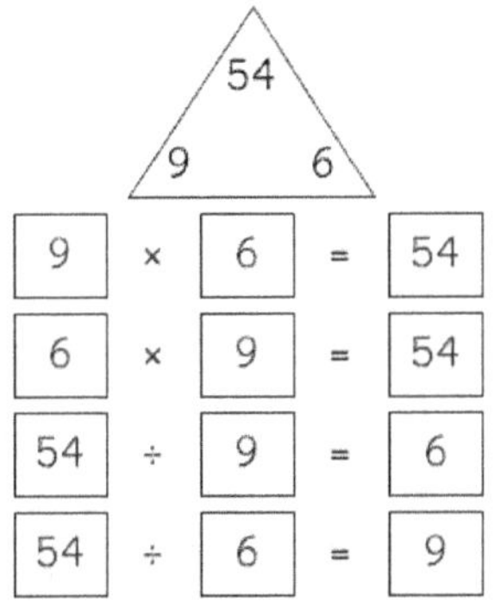

9	×	6	=	54
6	×	9	=	54
54	÷	9	=	6
54	÷	6	=	9

487. 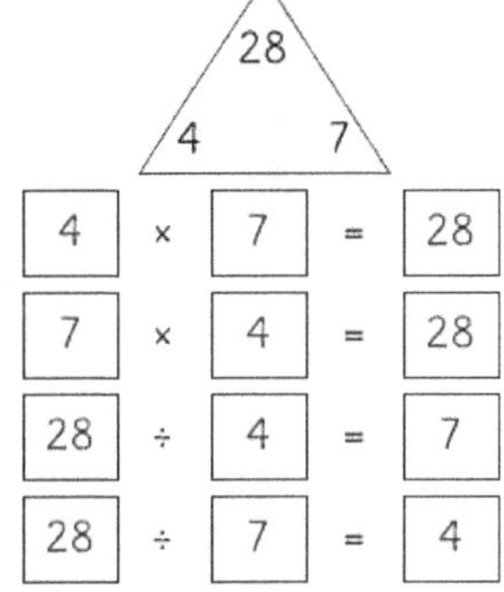

4	×	7	=	28
7	×	4	=	28
28	÷	4	=	7
28	÷	7	=	4

488. 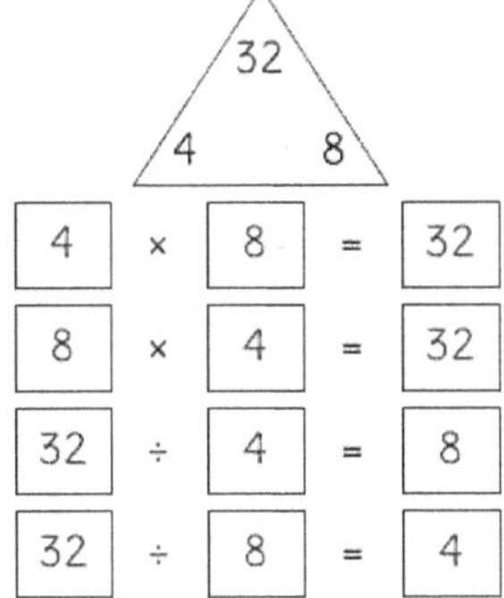

4	×	8	=	32
8	×	4	=	32
32	÷	4	=	8
32	÷	8	=	4

489. 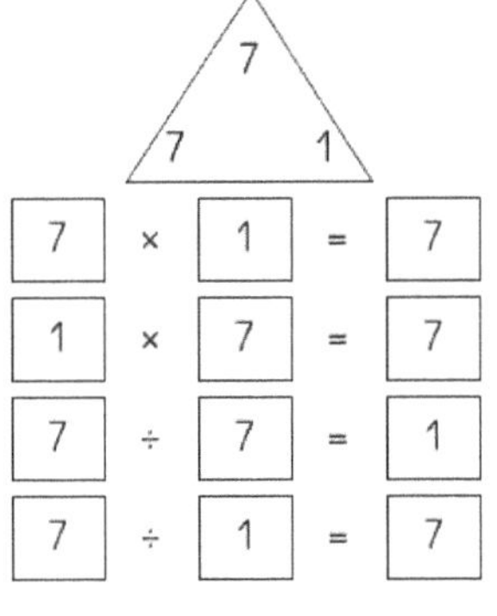

7	×	1	=	7
1	×	7	=	7
7	÷	7	=	1
7	÷	1	=	7

490. 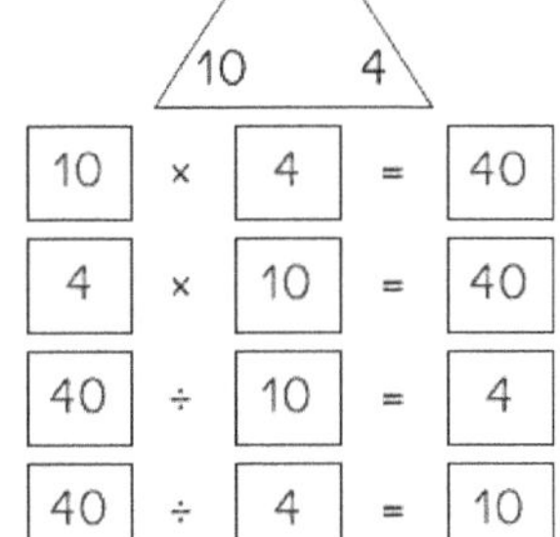

10	×	4	=	40
4	×	10	=	40
40	÷	10	=	4
40	÷	4	=	10

491.

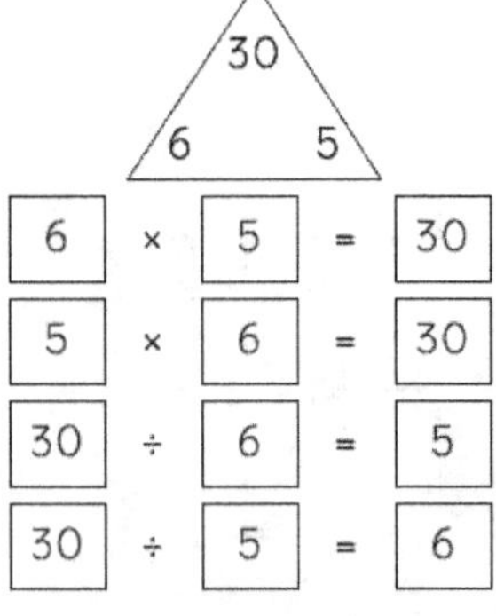

6	×	5	=	30
5	×	6	=	30
30	÷	6	=	5
30	÷	5	=	6

492.

7	×	4	=	28
4	×	7	=	28
28	÷	7	=	4
28	÷	4	=	7

493.

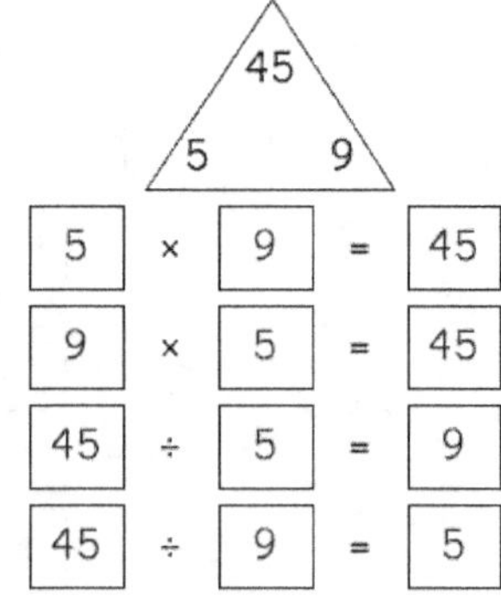

5	×	9	=	45
9	×	5	=	45
45	÷	5	=	9
45	÷	9	=	5

494.

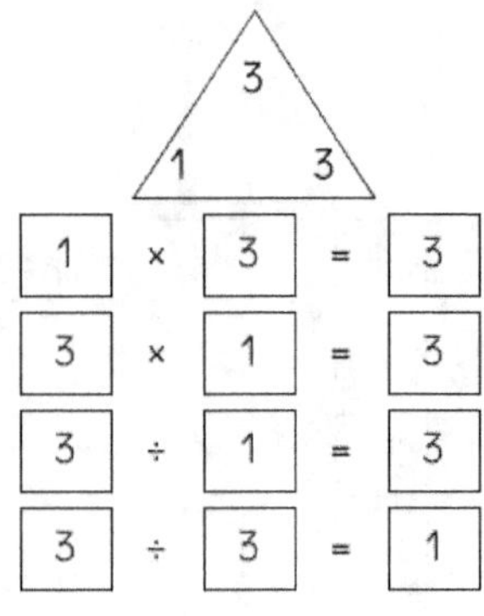

1	×	3	=	3
3	×	1	=	3
3	÷	1	=	3
3	÷	3	=	1

495.

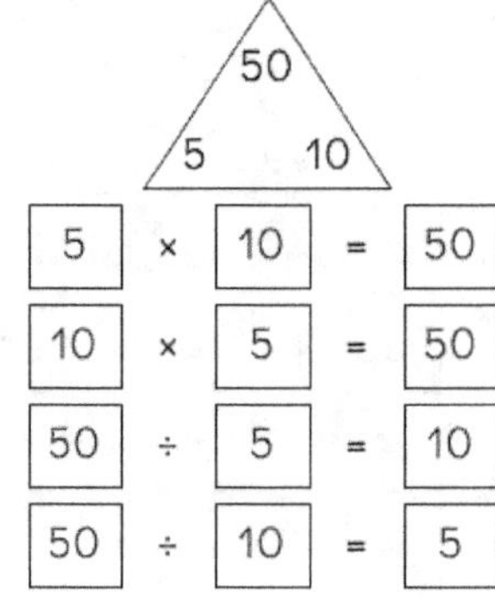

5	×	10	=	50
10	×	5	=	50
50	÷	5	=	10
50	÷	10	=	5

496.

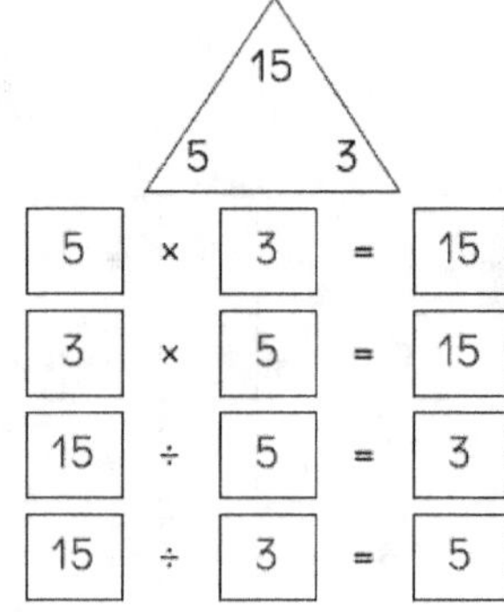

5	×	3	=	15
3	×	5	=	15
15	÷	5	=	3
15	÷	3	=	5

497.

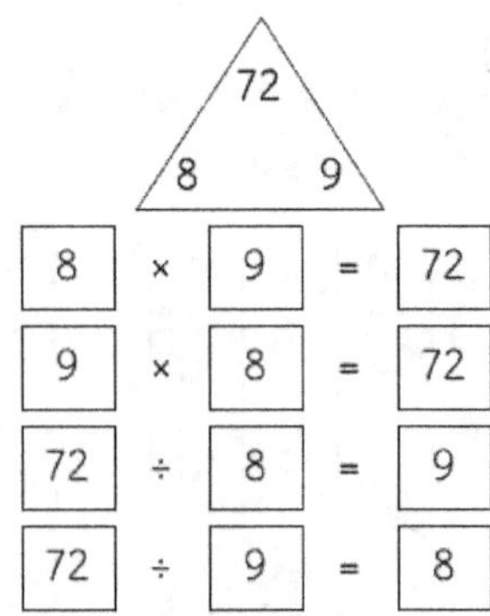

8	×	9	=	72
9	×	8	=	72
72	÷	8	=	9
72	÷	9	=	8

498.

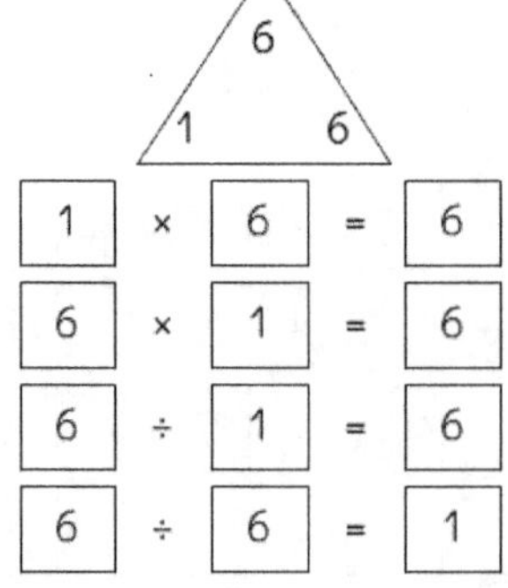

1	×	6	=	6
6	×	1	=	6
6	÷	1	=	6
6	÷	6	=	1

499.

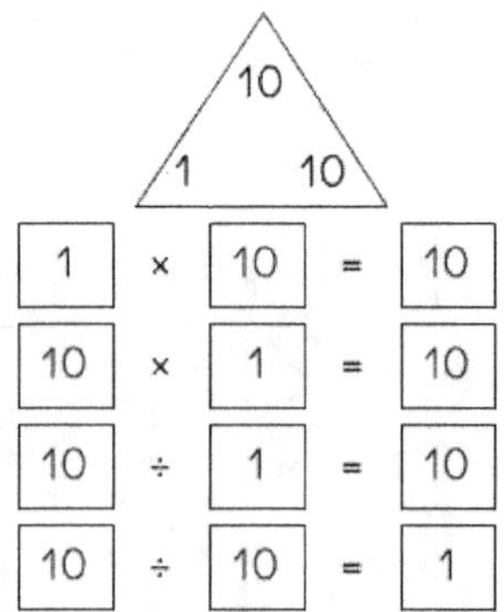

1	×	10	=	10
10	×	1	=	10
10	÷	1	=	10
10	÷	10	=	1

500. 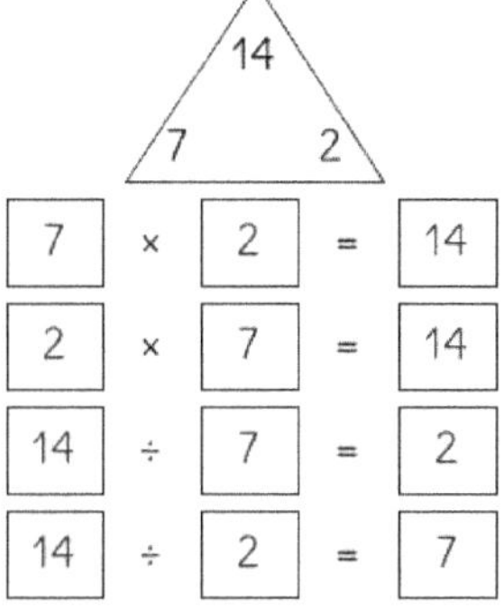

7	×	2	=	14
2	×	7	=	14
14	÷	7	=	2
14	÷	2	=	7

501.

3	×	5	=	15
5	×	3	=	15
15	÷	3	=	5
15	÷	5	=	3

502. 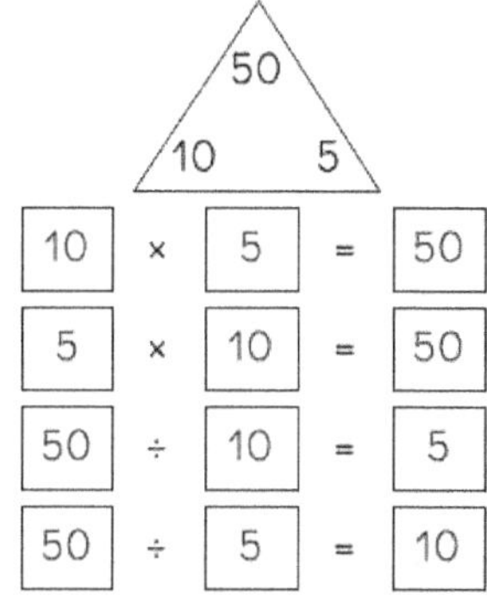

10	×	5	=	50
5	×	10	=	50
50	÷	10	=	5
50	÷	5	=	10

503. 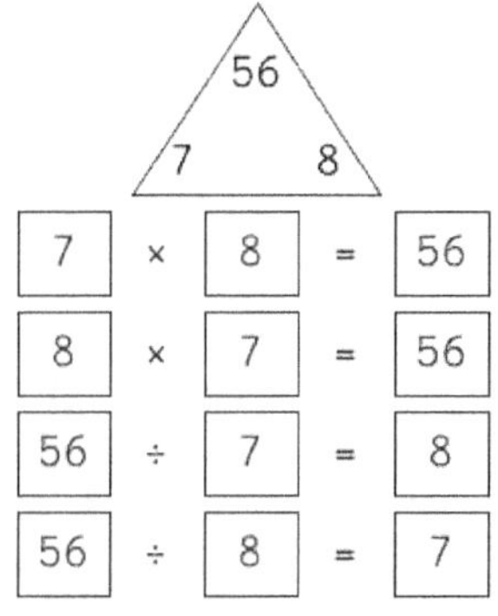

7	×	8	=	56
8	×	7	=	56
56	÷	7	=	8
56	÷	8	=	7

504. 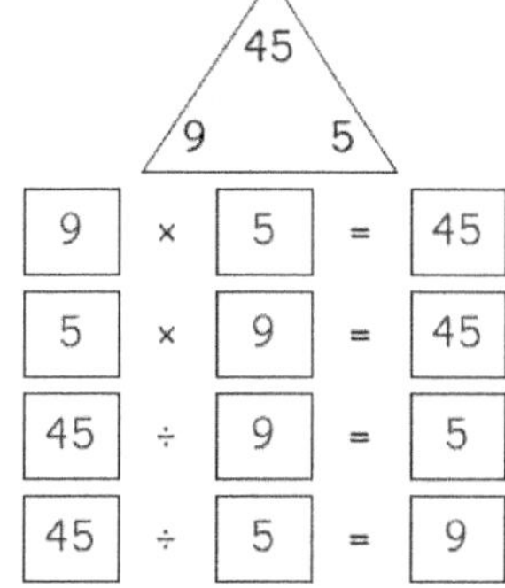

9	×	5	=	45
5	×	9	=	45
45	÷	9	=	5
45	÷	5	=	9

505. 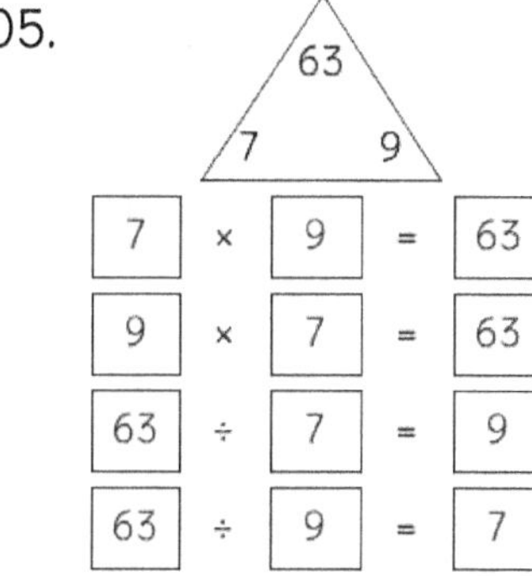

7	×	9	=	63
9	×	7	=	63
63	÷	7	=	9
63	÷	9	=	7

506. 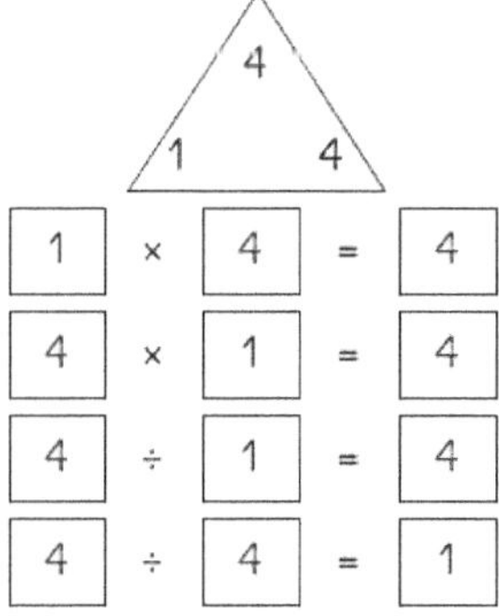

1	×	4	=	4
4	×	1	=	4
4	÷	1	=	4
4	÷	4	=	1

507. 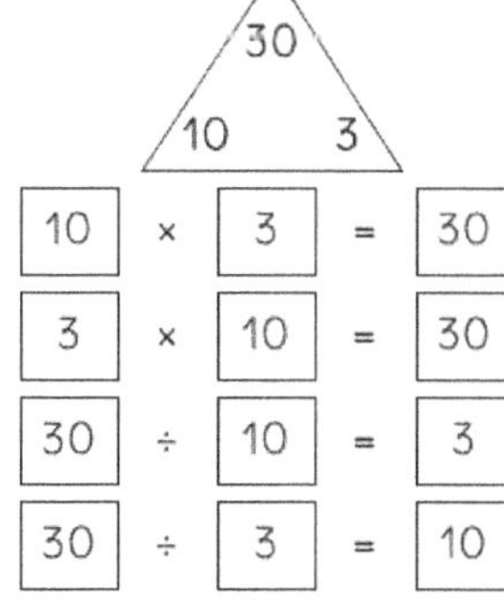

10	×	3	=	30
3	×	10	=	30
30	÷	10	=	3
30	÷	3	=	10

508. 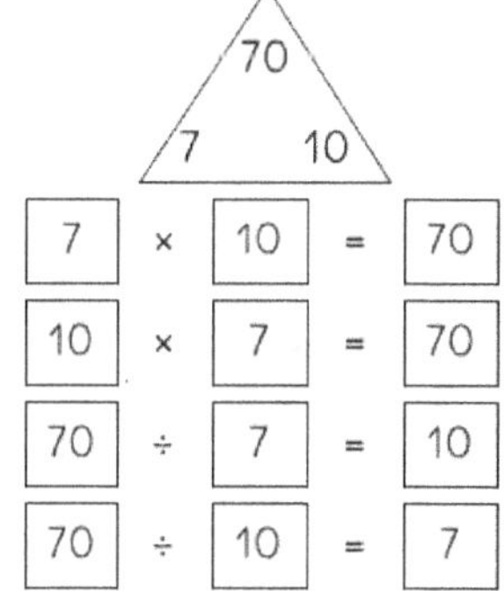

7	×	10	=	70
10	×	7	=	70
70	÷	7	=	10
70	÷	10	=	7

509. 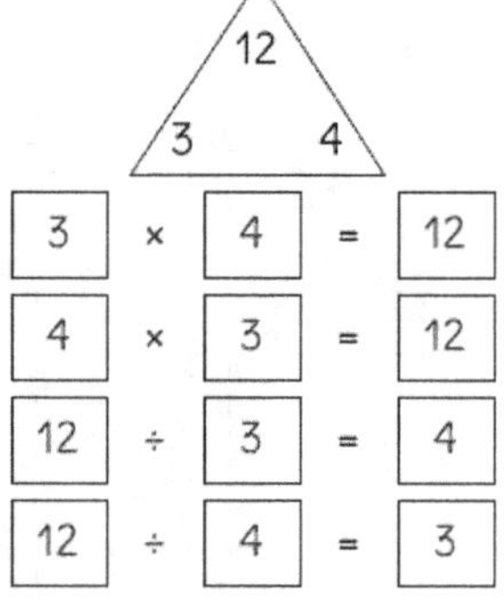

3	×	4	=	12
4	×	3	=	12
12	÷	3	=	4
12	÷	4	=	3

510. 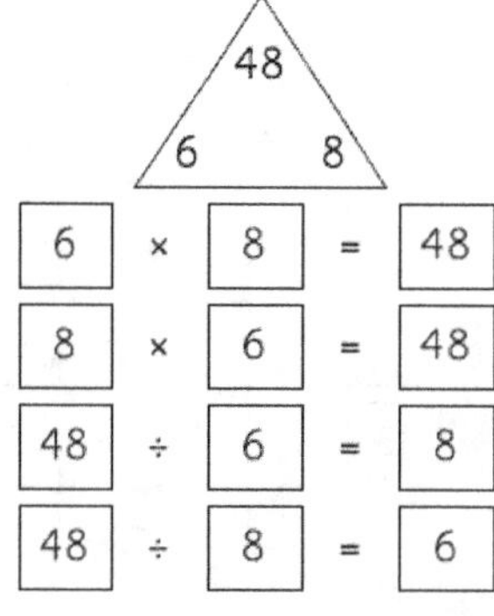

6	×	8	=	48
8	×	6	=	48
48	÷	6	=	8
48	÷	8	=	6

511. 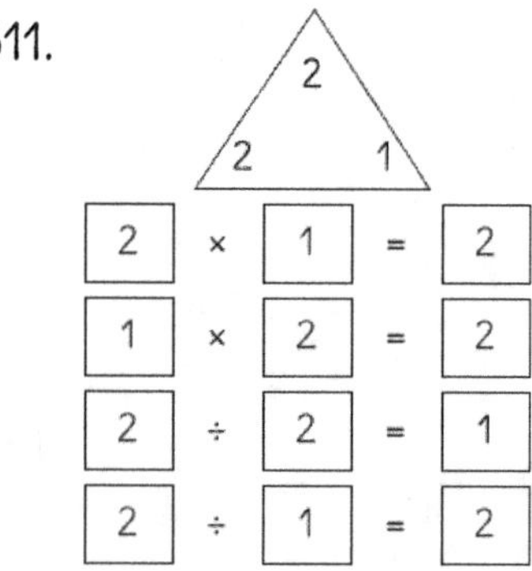

2	×	1	=	2
1	×	2	=	2
2	÷	2	=	1
2	÷	1	=	2

512. 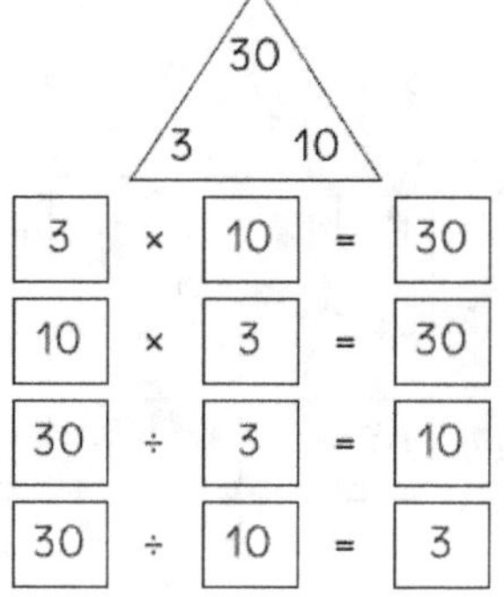

3	×	10	=	30
10	×	3	=	30
30	÷	3	=	10
30	÷	10	=	3

513. 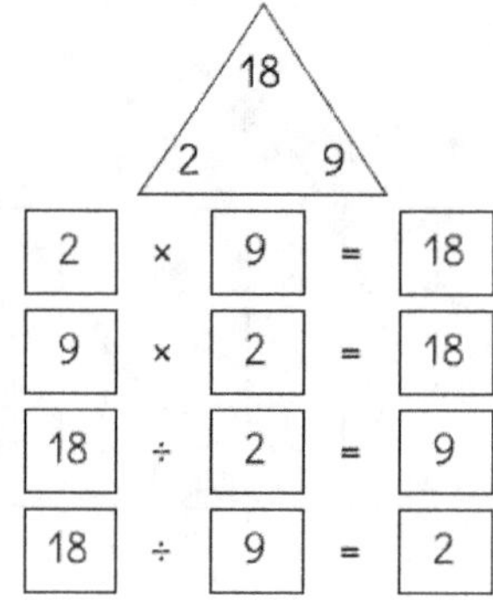

2	×	9	=	18
9	×	2	=	18
18	÷	2	=	9
18	÷	9	=	2

514. 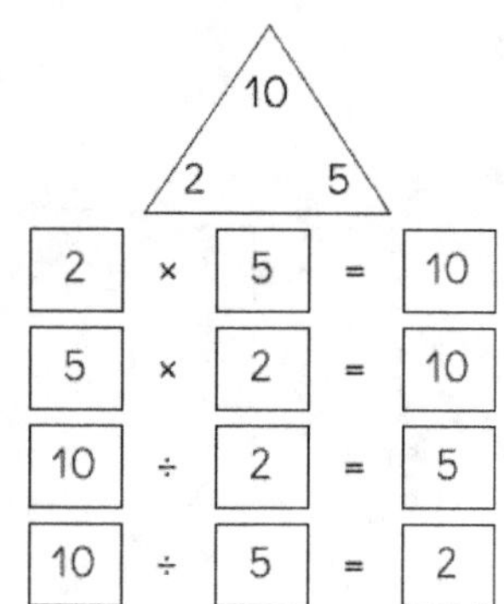

2	×	5	=	10
5	×	2	=	10
10	÷	2	=	5
10	÷	5	=	2

515. 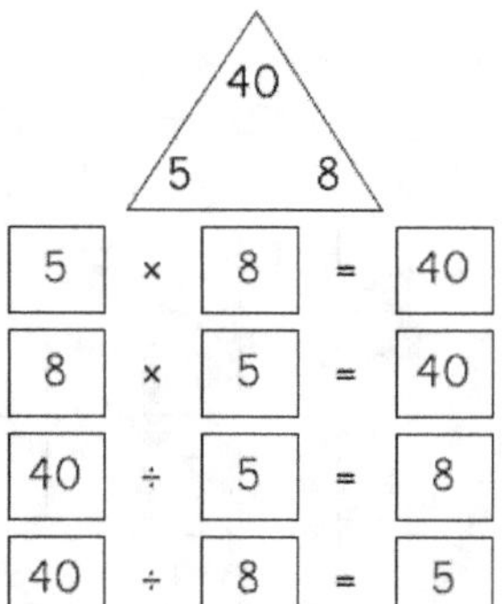

5	×	8	=	40
8	×	5	=	40
40	÷	5	=	8
40	÷	8	=	5